THE
MENSA
Book of Words,
WORD GAMES,
Puzzles & Oddities

THE
MENSA
Book of Words,
WORD GAMES,
Puzzles & Oddities

DR. ABBIE F. SALNY

GALAHAD BOOKS
NEW YORK

Copyright © 1988 by Dr. Abbie F. Salny.

First Galahad Books edition published in 2000.

Galahad Books
A division of BBS Publishing Corporation
386 Park Avenue South
New York, NY 10016

Galahad Books is a registered trademark of
BBS Publishing Corporation.

This edition published by arrangement with
HarperCollins Publishers.

Library of Congress Catalog Card Number: 99-75366

ISBN: 1-57866-082-3

Designer: C. Linda Dingler

Printed in the United States of America.

CONTENTS

To Jerry Salny, as always, and to fellow Mensans Roberta Rubin, M.D., and Barnett Zumoff, M.D., for helpful words.

FOREWORD

This book is about the glories and delights of my language, English. Despite the Eastern European origin of my name, I am an Englishman. English is the language I speak, the language I use as an author, and the language I love. English is part of all our customs and culture, and the customs and culture that foster the language in turn are part of our world heritage. It is this heritage that lends richness and strength to our language, not because English is pure and homogenous, but because it is an eclectic and heterogeneous selection of the best from many sources. And in its turn English has come to influence its many sources: because of the enormous world influence of Anglophone peoples, the British Empire, and more recently America and other members of the Commonwealth, English is rapidly becoming a lingua franca. It is the first-choice second language the world over.

My second great love is for the organization that has enabled me to discover a higher loyalty to the world culture shared and contributed to by eighty thousand members worldwide: Mensa. This world culture is the system of knowledge, know-how, skills, arts, science and technology, commercial practice, style of communication and cooperation that educated and intelligent people everywhere share.

As a great Mensan, Dr. Abbie Salny has a place of particular importance in this culture. She is one of the few enthusiasts who keep our strange ship afloat. As a very able and well-trained psychometric psychologist, she was of inestimable use to me in my long years as Mensa's International Chairman. Without her world travel and assiduous work in many lands,

Mensa would not have spread so far in and beyond the Anglophone world.

In this delightful, perceptive, and most importantly, *fun* etymology, Abbie takes us on an adventurous journey around the varied and unexpected sources of the language we all delight in using. Your understanding of the rich subtleties of English and your joy in its beauty will be greatly enhanced by this book.

—Victor Serebriakoff
Honorary International
President of Mensa

INTRODUCTION

Since this is a Mensa book of words, word origins, derivations, meanings, and oddities, perhaps we should begin by defining the word "Mensa"—or rather, by saying what "Mensa" is not. It is not an acronym or a slang Spanish expression. Nor is it the word for student dining hall, although it is used this way in some European countries. It is not even an obscure or foreign word for genius. "Mensa" *is* the Latin word for table and the name of an international society composed exclusively of individuals who have scored in the top 2 percent on any standard intelligence test (or its equivalent). When two barristers, the late Roland Berrill and Dr. Launcelot Lionel Ware, O.B.E., founded and named the organization more than forty years ago in Oxford, England, they envisioned a round table of equals with members from around the world. It is interesting to note that the design for the Mensa emblem features a slightly misshapen *M* forming a square table, with a globe floating somewhat precariously above it: an excellent symbol for a somewhat amorphous group, speaking dozens of languages, with no coherent philosophy, linked only by high scores on IQ tests.

Under the long-term direction of the now honorary president, Victor Serebriakoff, an almost irrepressible enthusiast and promoter of Mensa, the organization has grown to nearly 80,000 members around the world with, to paraphrase the old joke, at least 80,001 opinions. Although the Mensa Constitution strictly forbids Mensa itself from expressing an opinion, like-minded Mensans have formed Special Interest Groups (SIGs) to exchange ideas, usually by mail. At last count we found a listing of over 150 SIGs, including Astronomy and Space, the Libertarians, the Millard Fillmore Association, the Shyness SIG, the Skydiving SIG, the Soul SIG, Over 80, the Civil Liberties SIG, and so on.

The question that any Mensan who is interviewed by anyone must be prepared to face is, "Well, how can you justify such an elitist organization?" There's only one answer to that loaded question. Any organization with an admission criterion is elitist. The fact that Mensa has only one criterion, whether you live in Lagos, London, or Los Angeles, or even Ladakh, makes it less elitist than most membership organizations. Rank, money, social standing, occupation, race, sex, and skin color are totally irrelevant. All that matters is a score in the top 2 percent on any standard IQ test.

Despite popular opinion, not all Mensa meetings are intellectual. There may be family picnics, cruises, "fold, staple, and mutilate" parties (at which the rather onerous task of putting together several hundred newspapers for the local group is turned into an occasion for fun mixed with hard work), a Great Books discussion, a local theater-going group, a games evening, an impromptu party in honor of a visiting Mensan, a lunch group (one of which has gathered once a month for twenty-two years), or an evening of table-hopping, eating, and drinking at a local (tolerant) restaurant.

Above all, Mensans love to use words, and the propensity of Mensans to write, speak, and, in general, to use words, is apparent in many Mensa activities. The local newspapers for each Mensa group, the national magazine that goes to every Mensan, and the publicity for Mensa all tend to feature words, word puzzles, word games, and a great deal of correspondence. For those isolated by geography or for any other reason, there is the "little green rag," fondly known to its readers around the world as *The Isolated M,* a member-to-member service. The "little green rag" also features, to the expressed dismay of new readers, things called feghoots, after the title of the book in which they originally appeared. Feghoots are somewhat spooneristic puns. Typical is the story of the two little Swiss boys riding down an Alp, with their mother on the handlebars. After one sharp curve, the first brother says to the second, "Look Hans, no Ma!" No Mensa gathering is complete without a few new feghoots although, admittedly, there are those who hate them passionately.

The range of members is wide. Computer whiz Sir Clive Sinclair is, among many other things, chairman of British Mensa. Isaac Asimov, the noted, prolific polyglot author, is honorary vice-president of International Mensa. Among other wordsmiths of one variety or another are Jean Auel, the best-selling author of the *Clan of the Cave Bear* series; Warren Murphy, up in the multimillion sales in many languages on the *Destroyer* series, and also the author of the screen version of *The Eiger Sanction* and coauthor of some prize-winning detective books; Rebecca Brandywine, the author of many popular romances; William Windom, the actor; Theodore Bikel; and Mensa's honorary president, Victor Serebriakoff. Experts in other fields include Donald Peterson of the Ford Motor Company; the charming lady known as Morocco, who happens to hold several graduate degrees in Middle-Eastern studies and Gypsy folklore, but may be best known for her Middle-Eastern dancing; the British-born engineer who holds the credit for some rather notable achievements in the oil industry, including the famous dry hole gravel island off the North Slope of Alaska. She even has a ship named for her.

While all the thousands of jobs listed in the government manuals may not be represented, Mensa does have postal employees, one of whom fills lecture halls regularly when he speaks on Sherlock Holmes. We also have a world-renowned cancer specialist; a lawyer who obtained her degree at an age when many of us are thinking of retirement, and then became a successful member of a law firm; and many, many more from all walks of life. Many are polymaths who have deliberately chosen to live low-key lives at work in order to pursue their many other interests. The world may not call them "successful," but they live rich lives and consider themselves both successful and happy—and Mensa welcomes all of them.

Perhaps the most endearing feature of Mensa is the generosity of its members to other members. It is possible for a member to lose his job, send notes to half a dozen Mensa newsletters in the United States and abroad, and wind up not only with a job but with a temporary place to live while getting settled and a ready-made network of friends. Mensa newsletters often contain thank-you notes indicating that the recipient has had help offered in an emergency, an illness, or a death. It is this sense of extended family that seems to glue together the members of the society, and this sense of "belonging" that keeps Mensans renewing their membership. Unless, of course, they have become life members and know that they are part of the group forever.

1

WORDS, WORDS, AND MORE WORDS

Perhaps you have a poinsettia plant adorning your house, or you might have seen the beautiful bougainvillea that grows in the tropics. You've probably had your silhouette drawn at a fair or an amusement park. But do you know why or how each of them acquired its name? Louis Antoine de Bougainville was the first Frenchman to circumnavigate the globe. He brought home the pretty flowers and they've been known by his name ever since. But silhouette? and Poinsettia? You'll have to read on and find out about them. Why, for example, is a taboo called a taboo? It's the title of a very famous book, *Totem and Tabu*, which most college students have to read. But why taboo (or tabu)? We talk about those who have studied in the groves of Academe or who those have been academicians, but why are they called that? You'll find the answer in this chapter, and you may be very surprised!

If you have ever seen a vaudeville show—on television or in the movies—or if there was a theater in your town, many years ago, named the Vaudeville, you may have wondered where it got its name. On a less happy note, shrapnel is well known to soldiers unfortunate enough to come into contact with it. But why "shrapnel"? Who gave it its name? You will find that out too by carefully reading this chapter. (But we will tell you right now that a harlot was originally a knave, and male!)

Many of the more common derivations that you can find in any textbook have been intentionally omitted here. But in this chapter you *will* find the odd, the unusual, the unexpected, and even the startling.

So test yourself on the questions first. See how much you really do know about the ways our language grew and developed. Then check your answers; and find out the odd twists, turns, and allegorical ideas that have crept in over the years during which the Old English of the Saxons was overlaid with German, with Norman French, with Latin, and with Greek, to create the amalgam we call English today.

But remembering your Latin roots isn't going to be much help either. In a particularly fiendish manner, we have carefully omitted those words which have come down directly from the Latin prefixes and suffixes many of us had to memorize in school. There aren't many "ex = from" in this book. Instead, there are a good many invented words here. Shakespeare is reputed to have made up several hundred words all by himself. Not all of them have survived, and several were printer's errors in transcription, but many words sprang direct from his fertile and inventive brain, and some are included here.

Customs have changed, language has changed: now an afternoon show, matinee was once a morning performance; its root is *matin*, which means "morning." How about noon? That one may surprise you.

In short, or reasonably short, English is full of interesting surprises. Here you will find several hundred such surprising words, with derivations that are not only *not* obvious, but rather unusual. The words have been picked to inform, educate, and amuse. Some will lead you down the primrose path of misdirection, some are straightforward when you think of them, and some are obscure. All will provide you with an interesting vocabulary and fill your storehouse of odd facts and ideas. Each word will give you a small insight into the odd ways in which the human mind works. The connections are clear, once you see them, but totally invisible until you ponder them. Enjoy!

There are many derivations, with which we are all familiar, that have passed into common usage. Most people know that macadam comes from the name of the man who invented it. But did he also popularize the macadamia nut? Read on and find out. There is a folklore story about the guillotine. Is it true? The facts are given in this chapter. Astonish yourself, amaze your friends, and learn the true meaning of words you use every day. Take the quiz that follows and see how much you really know about common, ordinary words with quite extraordinary backgrounds and derivations.

1. **ACADEMY**   A place of learning, a group of learned men (people), like the French Academy
   a. From the Greek Plato's Academy, based on the Greek word meaning learned
   b. From Plato's last name, as his school was named after him
   c. From Akademos (or Academos), the owner of the area that Plato rented, where he held his school
2. **ADMIRAL**   Usually, the chief commander of a navy
   a. From Old French, meaning "to admire"
   b. From John Admiralis, an early English sea lord who was responsible for founding the British Navy
   c. From Arabic *amir al-bahr*, meaning "Lord of the Sea"
3. **AGNOSTIC**   One who believes that we know nothing beyond material phenomena. Often used as a description of someone who does not believe in the existence of a Supreme Being
   a. Used since the days of the Greek philosophers to describe someone who believes only that which he can see
   b. Originally used as the name for a nonreligious group founded in the Middle Ages in secrecy for fear of being charged as heretics, but eventually an acknowledged society

    c. A coined word, made up by T. H. Huxley in 1869 from the Greek roots meaning, more or less, "not knowing"

4. **ALGEBRA** A method of calculating by symbols

    a. From Pythagoras, who developed geometry and algebra and gave them their names

    b. From the initial steps originally used to calculate algebraic formulas; now disused, but originally taught as basic principles

    c. From Arabic *al-djabr*, "to put together something that was broken"—therefore a combination—from the verb *djabara*, "to reunite"

5. **ALIBI** A generalized excuse

    a. From the Latin, meaning "I was elsewhere"

    b. From a corruption of an early court term meaning "to plead 'Not Guilty' "

    c. From the Latin, meaning "I did not do this thing"

6. **AMETHYST** A bluish-violet quartz

    a. From the Greek word for that particular color

    b. From the Greek words meaning antidrunkenness, as it was supposed to prevent intoxication

    c. From the name of a Latin goddess, patroness of precious stones

7. **AMOK** To run wild

    a. A made-up word, an acronym for *A* *M*ad *O*ld *K*iller, used in English courts for mass murderers

    b. From Malay, *amoq*, meaning "frenzied"

    c. Old Norse, a term applied to the warriors who went out with the express intention of cutting down anyone who stood in the way of their conquests

8. **ANTIMACASSAR** A covering for chair and sofa backs

    a. A particular knit stitch developed during Queen Victoria's time for such coverings and transferred to the coverings themselves, which are often knitted or crocheted

    b. Derived from Mr. Macassar, a noted bon vivant of the seventeenth century, who used so much hair oil that it was necessary for society hostesses to have special coverings anywhere he might rest his head

c. From macassar oil, commonly used for hair dressing, but quite greasy and tending to stain chair backs and sofa backs

9. **APERIENT** A form of drink
   a. Another word for an aperitif, or drink usually served before dinner to whet the appetite of the prospective diner
   b. A particularly bitter drink, as compared to the usual aperitif, which is often semisweet or, at most, slightly dry
   c. A laxative, from the Latin word meaning "to open"

10. **ARCTIC** Relating to the north; extremely cold
    a. From the star Arcturus, which the early astronomers knew was part of a constellation that pointed north
    b. Latin for an extremely cold place
    c. From the Greek word for bear

11. **ASSASSIN** A murderer, often used for political murders
    a. From Old French, meaning "to kill"
    b. From Arabic, meaning "he who kills for the glory of his country"
    c. From Iran, as a derivative of a particular sect that was supposed to commit murder under the influence of hashish, and was therefore called hashshashin

12. **ATLAS** A book of maps, plates, and geographical information; a mountain range in Africa
    a. Atlas was the Titan who bore the heavens on his shoulders, so any representation of the heavens or the Earth was named after him
    b. Atlas's picture appeared on the first widely sold book of maps, and people got into the habit of calling it "the Atlas," whence the name was transferred to all books of maps
    c. From the Greek word meaning "to support" and, by extension, to support the world

13. **AURORA** The dawn; a rich orange color; a luminous meteoric phenomenon of the northern and southern polar regions
    a. From Latin Aurora, the goddess of the dawn
    b. From Latin, meaning "rosy glow," or the color involved
    c. From aura, as a back-formation: aura is a supposed subtle emanation, and by extension this term was enlarged to mean the emanation of light at dawn

14. **AZALEA**   A subgenus of Rhododendron
   a.   From Simeon Azael, a Middle-Eastern botanist (1563–1616) who introduced the plant to Europe
   b.   From the Old English, meaning a plant that grows in flat areas (lea)
   c.   From the Greek word meaning "dry," as it was believed to grow best in dry soil

15. **BADMINTON**   A game played with shuttlecocks
   a.   The Hindu word for shuttlecock, which the British acquired when they learned the game in India
   b.   Old English for a similar game played in medieval times
   c.   From Badminton Castle, home of the duke of Gloucester, where the game seems to have originated

16. **BAGATELLE**   A trifle, a small nothing
   a.   From the Bagatelle Palace in the Bois de Boulogne in Paris, which is a tiny, miniature palace built in a very short time on a bet
   b.   From the Old French, meaning "a small building"
   c.   Old French or Italian, meaning a conjuror's trick or trifle

17. **BALDACHIN (or BALDAQUIN)**   A canopy over a throne or pulpit (like the magnificent and famous one at St. Peter's Cathedral in Rome)
   a.   Architectural term for such a covering, originally of wood or stone
   b.   Latin word meaning "covering"
   c.   From Italian, originally Baldacco, or Baghdad, where the cloth for such a canopy was made

18. **BALLOT**   A means of voting
   a.   Named for the small box into which ballots were originally dropped
   b.   Named for the inventor of this means of voting—dropping marked copies of an election choice into a box—instead of public hand-raising, Johannus Balotinus
   c.   From the Italian for "small ball," as formerly ballots were cast by dropping white balls into a box for yes, and black balls into the same box for a no vote

19. **BARBARIAN** Originally one who was neither Greek nor Roman, an uncouth person without taste or refinement
   a. From the Greek *barbaros*, literally, "stammering," derived from the odd sounds foreigners made
   b. From the Latin word for beard—as the foreigners tended to be bearded, like the noted warrior Frederick Barbarossa
   c. From a foreign tribe of extremely rough savages, the Barbarians, who invaded Greece in 600 B.C.

20. **BASCULE** A type of bridge in which a weight at one end is lowered in order to raise the other end
   a. From Pierre Bascule, who invented this type of bridge during the Hundred Years' War, to keep enemies from crossing a river without forcing the defenders to blow up the bridge, so they could still use it at some future time
   b. From the French word for seesaw, as that is what the bridge's action resembles
   c. From a misunderstanding of a different term in engineering, so that it developed as folk etymology ("sparrowgrass" for "asparagus" is a type of folk etymology)

21. **BEDLAM** A madhouse, a place of uproar
   a. A corruption of Babel, the tower where everyone spoke a different language, which sounded mad
   b. From the priory of St. Mary of Bethlehem in London, which later became a madhouse
   c. From Sir Thomas Bedlam, a noted physician of medieval England who fought for humane care of the insane

22. **BIBLE** Usually, the sacred writings of Judaism or the Christian church, consisting of the Old and (for Christians) the New Testaments—by extension, any sacred writings
   a. From Greek *biblios*, "books," originally meaning "papyrus"
   b. From the name given to those writings by the early prophets
   c. From the description used by manuscript writers who copied them by hand

23. **BLAZER**   A type of sports jacket, originally worn only by men
   a. From the fact that the originals were always blazing red, and the name came to be applied to any jacket of that type
   b. From the Earl of Blazer, a friend of Beau Brummel, who popularized the style for hunting jackets
   c. From Blaezera, in northern India, where the British officers first had these loose cotton jackets made to save them from the discomfort of the tight, fitted regimental jackets worn on duty

24. **BOWDLERIZE**   To clean up literary material, to censor, usually in an unnecessary sense
   a. From the name of Dr. T. Bowdler (1754–1825), who decided to expurgate Shakespeare and took out everything that "could bring a blush to the cheek" when he published a new edition
   b. From Middle English, meaning "to expurgate"
   c. From the German, meaning "to scrub" or "clean"

25. **BOYCOTT**   An organized refusal to deal with a person or business firm
   a. A slang term made up in the early days of the nineteenth century, when there were racial problems in various parts of the United States
   b. From Captain Charles Boycott, a land agent in Ireland who made himself so unpopular that after having his life protected by British soldiers, he was forced to move. The "boycott" was totally effective
   c. Origin unknown

26. **BUNKUM**   Bombastic speechmaking that is really not intended for the audience, but is actually meant to be read elsewhere to make the speaker sound important; also nonsense or humbug
   a. From bunko, meaning a confidence game or a trickster
   b. Allegedly from a senator who spoke at length in Congress and, when reproved for the length of his speeches and their irrelevancies, said that he was just speaking for the record in Buncombe County (his constituency)

c. William H. Bunkum, a long-winded, bombastic senator, the butt of many jokes for his nonsense speeches

27. **BURNOUT** A common expression meaning that the person involved has lost interest in whatever it is he or she is doing—as in such expressions as "volunteer burnout"
   a. From the point in the flight of a rocket when the rocket engine's fuel runs out
   b. From the original use of the word, meaning "entirely consumed"
   c. Origin and earliest use in current sense unknown

28. **CABOCHON** A gem, usually precious, cut rounded on top and flat on the back, without facets
   a. From the jeweler L. M. Cabochon, who developed this cut originally
   b. From the French for half-rounded, to describe the shape
   c. From the Latin, meaning "head," in other words, that there was no back to the stone and only the head showed

29. **CALCULATE** To count or reckon; to think out or think through, especially with regard to mathematics
   a. From the Greek word meaning "to count," *kalyx*
   b. From the root meaning "to add together," occurring in many early languages
   c. From the Latin word *calculus,* "little stone"

30. **CAMELLIA** A genus of evergreen closely akin to tea, noted for their beautiful flowers; and the shrub of this name
   a. From Latin *camellus,* as the leaves have a hump resembling that of a camel
   b. From the town Camelot in England, where they were first introduced to the Western world
   c. From the Moravian Jesuit priest Kamel, who collected the plant in the Philippine Islands

31. **CATECHISM** Any organized system of teaching drawn up on the question-and-answer basis
   a. This name was given to religious instruction by the early Hebrews—meaning "religious teachings"

     b.   From the name given to this style of teaching and learning by the philosopher Catechismus of the University of Bologna in the fourteenth century

     c.   Via Latin, from the Greek roots of "sound" and "back," forming a Greek word meaning "to din into the ears"

32. **CHAUVINISM**   Pride in one's country carried to a ridiculous degree, coupled with contempt for other groups or nations

     a.   From Nicolas Chauvin, a veteran of the Napoleonic Wars, who was made a public figure by his caricature in a play of the times

     b.   From the French, meaning "patriotism," basically, love of one's country

     c.   Origin unknown

33. **CHESS**   A game of skill, with varying figures, played by two players on a board with checkered squares

     a.   From the Old French, meaning "war games"

     b.   From Guillaume Chessier, who developed the game from its Near Eastern origin

     c.   Originally from Persian *shah,* meaning "king," which is the most powerful figure on the board

34. **CHICANERY**   Common usage is trickery or deceit, especially at law

     a.   From a legal term meaning deceitful practices

     b.   From the Persian word *tchuagun,* meaning a crooked mallet

     c.   From a Norman French lawyer, Nicolas Chicane (1140–1183), who was noted for winning all of his cases by the use of some trick or ruse in the presentation of evidence or the interviewing of witnesses

35. **CLINK**   Slang word for prison

     a.   From the sound the door makes when it shuts behind the prisoner

     b.   From the clinking sounds of the chains attached to the ankles of the prisoners

     c.   From the Clink Prison on Clink Street in Southwark, London

36. **CLOCK** A machine for measuring time, now commonly with a dial and hands showing the hours and minutes
   a. From the Latin word meaning "the measurement of time"
   b. From the sound of the ticking—poetically giving the sound as "clock, clock, clock"
   c. From the Late Latin, meaning "a bell"

37. **COACH** A vehicle; a private cabin; a motor bus; a four-wheeled special private carriage, usually for state occasions, and the like; a motorcar body
   a. From Old English, meaning a vehicle drawn by a team of horses
   b. From the French *caché*, meaning "hidden," as the occupants were hidden from view
   c. From the Hungarian Kocs, the town where these vehicles seem to have been made originally

38. **COBALT** A metallic element, of atomic number 27
   a. From the name of the color, after which it was named
   b. From German *Kobold*, a demon. The miners believed that the metal was dangerous and that the mines or the metal were activated by the spirit of these little demons
   c. From the discoverer of this element, Nicholas Coball (1871–1903), who had it named after him following his early death from exposure to Cobalt 60, a radioactive form

39. **COFFEE** Now, the powder made from grinding the coffee bean; the drink made from this powder
   a. From the Arabic *kahwah*, originally meaning wine but then meaning coffee, via the Turkish
   b. From the discoverer of the coffee plant, Li Kah-Fee, about 1100, in China
   c. From the English, via the name of the tavern owned by John Coffee, where the beverage was first served to the public

40. **COPPER** A metal, atomic number 29
   a. From the Latin, meaning "shiny"
   b. From the caves of Cooperium, in Turkey, where the metal was first identified

    c. From Latin, derived from *cyprium*, because it was originally found in Cyprus

41. **CURFEW** Now, commonly, a regulation requiring persons to be indoors at a certain time

    a. From Old English, meaning "to lock doors"

    b. From Old French, meaning "to cover a fire," and in medieval times the ringing of a bell signaling the time to extinguish all lights and fires

    c. English legal term regarding the right of the State to regulate travel in the streets

42. **d** Just as printed, an abbreviation for the British penny, as in £, S, d for pounds, shillings, and pence (the new currency system uses pennies and pounds on a decimal system)

    a. Originally abbreviated in this manner to avoid confusion with pounds, the money unit

    b. To avoid confusion with pounds, the unit of weight

    c. From the Latin *denarius*

43. **DAGUERREOTYPE** A type of photography on copper plates; word used generically for many early photographs

    a. From the French, meaning "etched image"

    b. From Louis Daguerre, who helped to invent and to opularize this type of photography in the nineteenth century

    c. From the town of Daguerre, France, where the first photographic film of this sort was manufactured

44. **DAHLIA** A Mexican genus of garden composites, with large, brightly colored flowers

    a. From the Spanish word meaning "brightly colored"

    b. Named by the famous Swedish botanist and taxonomist Linnaeus, after one of his students

    c. A native Mexican name for the plant, which was adopted when the plant was discovered

45. **DAMASK** A type of heavily patterned, woven cloth

    a. Named for the damask rose, which was the pattern always used originally

    b. Named for the inventor of the loom that wove that type of pattern, Petrus Damusk

    c.   Named for Damascus, where material like this seems to have been first woven

46.   **DELTA**   The mouth of a river; an alluvial deposit, usually at a river mouth

    a.   The Greek for "river mouth"

    b.   The geologic term for alluvial deposits of this type

    c.   From the Greek letter delta, shaped like a triangle, as the Nile Delta has that shape (many others do not); and the word, by extension, has come to be used for any river-mouth delta

47.   **DISASTER**   An adverse or unfortunate event; a great and sudden misfortune

    a.   From the Greek words meaning "falling from grace"

    b.   From Desastra, the Roman goddess of misfortune

    c.   From Greek, through Latin and French to current usage, via a Greek root meaning "a star," with an evil sense

48.   **DOILY (sometimes doyley)**   A piece of cloth; a small piece of cloth on a serving tray

    a.   From Old French meaning "lace cloth"

    b.   From a haberdasher, famous for his cloth, apparently English

    c.   Origin unknown—first appeared in a Shakespeare play, and he is known to have coined new words

49.   **DOLLAR**   A coin, usually worth one hundred cents, used as a unit of monetary value by many countries, including Canada, Australia, New Zealand, and the United States

    a.   Word invented during the American Revolution to distinguish American currency from that of Great Britain, which was not on the decimal system

    b.   From the German word *Joachimsthaler,* which passed into English as dollar

    c.   From the Latin *dolarius,* "payment"

50.   **DYNAMITE**   A powerful explosive

    a.   Name given to it by Alfred Nobel, who invented it

    b.   A rough approximation of the sound of the Chinese word meaning explosive, as it was used in China for many years prior to its development in Western countries

    c. From the Greek word *dynamos,* meaning "power"

51. **EARL** A British rank of nobleman, between a marquis and a viscount

    a. Title invented by William the Conqueror to reward his loyal followers after the Battle of Hastings

    b. First bestowed by Charles II to create a new level of courtiers who would be loyal to him

    c. From the Old English *eorl,* meaning "warrior"; originally from the Old Norse spoken by the Vikings

52. **ELEPHANT** A large mammal, of two general types, Indian and African, distinguished by its trunk and ears

    a. From the name given to it in India, which the early observers adopted as its name

    b. From the African word for "large beast that tramps through the jungle"

    c. Originally it was called by the same name as a camel, apparently on the theory that all exotic animals were the same

53. **ENEMY** One who hates or dislikes (as a noun); hating (as an adjective)

    a. From the Latin word meaning "the opposite of a friend"

    b. From Old English, meaning "hatred instilled by blood"

    c. Source unknown—appeared first in the King James translation of the Bible, as a substitute for the word *foe*

54. **ENGINEER** One who designs, makes, puts to practical use, or applies engines and other machines

    a. Developed when the steam engine came into use to describe the men who built them and the men who ran them

    b. From the French *ingénieur*

    c. By usage from the Latin word meaning "skill"

55. **ENIGMA** An obscure or hidden meaning; a puzzle

    a. One of the Greek "mysteries"; the protagonist of this drama with a hidden, obscure meaning

    b. From the Greek words meaning "to speak darkly" and "a fable"

    c. The name of a famous book in Old English literature; the first recorded mystery novel

56. **EPIDEMIC**   A plague, or other illness, affecting a large population
   a. From *epidermis,* meaning "skin," as the first signs of major illnesses such as leprosy showed themselves there
   b. From the Greek, originally *epi,* "among," and *demos,* "the people"
   c. From Epidemios, the minor god of panic and crowds, who was believed to be responsible for illnesses that affected large groups

57. **FACET**   A small surface, as of a crystal; or, as a verb, to cut into facets, for example, a diamond or other stone
   a. From the Latin *facere,* "to make"
   b. From the Latin for "small corner"
   c. From the same word as face, French *facette,* meaning "little face"

58. **FAHRENHEIT**   A thermometer with the freezing point of water at 32 degrees and the boiling point at 212 degrees
   a. From Old German *Fahren* and *Heit,* meaning measurement
   b. From Gabriel Fahrenheit (1686–1736), who developed this scale
   c. From the village in Germany where thermometers were first made

59. **FAUNA**   The assemblage of animals of a region or period
   a. From the Domesday Book—which started with listings of animals, including fawns, or fauns
   b. From the Old French meaning "ferns" or "plants" or "woods," where the animals lived
   c. From the Latin deities Fauna and Faunus, the patrons of those who keep animals

60. **FOMALHAUT**   A bright star in the constellation Southern Fish
   a. The name of the astronomer, Karl Fomalhaut (1690–1785), who discovered the constellation and named the star
   b. From Arabic words meaning "the whale's mouth"
   c. From the island of Fomalhaut in the South Pacific, where the star was first identified

61. **FORENSIC**   Belonging to courts of law
    a.   From the Latin word *Forum*, as that is where trials were held
    b.   From the Latin word meaning "to argue"
    c.   From Old French *forenne*, meaning "a judge" or "one who judges"

62. **FORUM**   A public meeting, a public discussion, a Roman city feature
    a.   From the Latin for "the common people," as that is where they met
    b.   From the Latin meaning "out-of-doors," as the forum was always an open space
    c.   From the Latin for "argument"

63. **FRANC**   A unit of currency, since 1795 the basis of French currency—now also a term used in Belgium, Switzerland, and elsewhere
    a.   From the Old French meaning "free," as exemplified by the Paris street called Franc-Bourgeois, or "free citizens"
    b.   From the French usage of the coin, any money from France used the adjective *franc*, which became the name of the money now so described
    c.   From the legend *francorum rex* on the coins when they were first minted, long before 1795

64. **GALAXY**   Without a capital *G* at the beginning, a luminous band of stars stretching across the heavens; a shining array
    a.   From the star Galactacus, the brightest star the ancients could see without a telescope
    b.   From the Greek word for milk and thus, by extension, both the Milky Way and similar assemblages of stars
    c.   From an early astronomer, Petrus Galax (al-Galax in Arabic)

65. **GAMBIT**   An opening move in chess; giving up something to gain an advantage—often used to mean a ploy
    a.   From the chess player Gambettus, who invented the technique
    b.   From Old Latin, meaning "to gamble" or to "wager"
    c.   From Italian, "a tripping up," from *gamba*, "leg"

66. **GARDENIA**   Old World genus of the madder family, with beautiful, fragrant flowers

   a. The most commonly grown flower in English gardens, hence known by that generic name

   b. From Dr. Alexander Garden (1730–1791), of the United States, who was a botanist

   c. From the Latin *gardenus*, meaning "fragrant garden flower"

67. **GAS**   A substance that has no fixed volume or space, but can expand; often one that is in this condition under normal terrestrial conditions (also the American contraction for "gasoline")

   a. A word invented by J. B. von Helmont (1577–1644), suggested by the Greek word *chaos*

   b. One of the six natural substances recognized by the Romans, which included earth, air, fire, and so on

   c. From the Greek god Kaseo, who represented space

68. **GERANIUM**   A group of plants that bear seeds resembling the beak of a certain species of bird

   a. Michael Geranus named it in 1653 when it was developed as a cross-bred hybrid from other plants in his garden

   b. From Greek and Latin *geranion/geranus*, "a crane," as it was thought that the seeds resembled a crane's bill

   c. From the Old English word for "small garden plant"

69. **GOURMET**   A connoisseur of fine food and drink

   a. From the French, meaning "food expert"

   b. From the French, meaning "a winemaker's assistant"

   c. From the French, meaning "fine tasting"

70. **GRAVITY**   Gravitational attraction; seriousness (when used figuratively)

   a. From the same root as *graven,* Latin for "engrave," meaning "to weigh in deeply," as in cutting a stone or metal

   b. A back-formation from "cavity," when the Earth was believed to be hollow and to attract falling objects into it

   c. From the Latin *gravitas*, "heavy"

71. **GUBERNATORIAL**   Pertaining to a governor
    a.   From *gubernor*, which has become "governor" by a vowel shift that often occurs
    b.   From the Spanish word for governor
    c.   From the Latin *gubernator*, "one who steers"

72. **GUILLOTINE**   A machine for beheading by the descent of a blade
    a.   Invented by Joseph Ignace Guillotin during the French Revolution and used on the inventor himself during that period
    b.   Its first use was during the French Revolution on Dr. Guillotin, and it was called thereafter by his name
    c.   Neither invented by nor used on Dr. Guillotin, but recommended by him as a more humane means of execution than the various forms of torture then in use

73. **GUNITE**   A mixture of cement and sand, finely graded cement concrete
    a.   Originally a trademarked name, used because the material was sprayed into place under air pressure by a cement gun
    b.   From the name of the manufacturer, Herman Gunnite (1908–1976)
    c.   From the Old English *gunariter,* meaning "to hold in place"

74. **HACIENDA**   An estate or ranch
    a.   From the Spanish for "country house"
    b.   From the Spanish-Portuguese for "to live in the country"
    c.   From the Spanish for "work to be done"

75. **HALCYON**   The kingfisher, a bird—or the figurative use of the word to mean calm, peaceful, and happy
    a.   The legend is that the kingfisher made a nest on the floating sea, which it calmed during hatching (from the Greek *alkyon,* fancifully changed to *halkyon,* meaning "sea" and "conceiving")
    b.   From the Greek word for "good fortune"
    c.   From the Latin, through a confusion with *alkyon* and *halkyon*

76. **HANSOM**   A type of light, two-wheeled cab, with the driver's seat behind (often met in Victorian literature)

   a. From the English "handsome," as the grooms who drove the cabs for wealthy families were selected for their fine looks

   b. From the inventor Joseph A. Hansom, 1803–1882

   c. From the fact that it was such a high carriage (as you can see from the illustrations of the time) that it was necessary to hand people in and out of the cab, as it was impossible to do so without a "hand" or assistance

77. **HAZARD**   An old dicing game; chance; accident

   a. Old French *hasard*, probably from Arabic *al-zahr*, the die; one story has it that it is from Hasart, a castle in Syria, where the game was invented during the Crusades

   b. From the croupier's last call to bet on a gaming wheel— "at hazard" before the bets are closed

   c. From a very popular board and dice game in France in the time of Louis XIV invented by Edouard Hasarde, duc de Beaucoup d'Argent

78. **HEAVISIDE LAYER**   A strongly ionized region about sixty miles up in the atmosphere, from which radio waves are reflected

   a. From the fact that this layer is so heavy that the waves bounce right back, not light like the rest of the atmosphere

   b. From O. Heaviside (and A. E. Kennelly) who inferred the existence of this layer originally; sometimes called the Kennelly-Heaviside layer

   c. There is a much lighter layer of atmosphere above it, the Lightside layer, and this was named in contrast

79. **KIOSK (sometimes KYOSK)**   A small pavilion for the sale of papers, candies, tickets, and so on, either inside or outside a building; a small roofed stall (in Britain, a telephone box)

   a. From the Old French *ciosce*, through the Italian, meaning "pavilion"

   b. From the Chicago World's Fair in 1892, where the word was invented for the gaily decorated small booths selling souvenirs

c.   From the Turkish, via Persian, *keushk,* a small pavilion located in a garden

80.   **KOWTOW**   To abase oneself, to show abasement before someone or something

a.   The Chinese word meaning "to knock the head," *k'o t'ou,* the mark of respect of touching forehead to floor

b.   Japanese for obeisance

c.   A corruption of bow, in the sense of inclining the head or lowering the upper part of the body, showing that the mark of respect was much deeper

81.   **LADY**   A woman, especially of refinement; the equivalent when capitalized of Lord, originally used for "wife," by upper-class women

a.   From the Latin *ladiusa,* meaning a high-born woman

b.   From Old English *ladye,* meaning the wife of a *lorde*

c.   From the Old English word, now lost, *dige,* coupled with *hlaef,* the whole word *hlaefdige* meaning "dough kneader"

82.   **LANTHANUM**   Metallic element, atomic number 57

a.   From the Latin *lantana,* "glowing," because it glows in the dark

b.   From the Greek *lanthanein,* "to escape notice," because it was hidden in rare minerals until 1839

c.   From its discoverer, John Lanthorn (1820–1901)

83.   **LARVA**   An animal in an immature but active state that differs markedly from an adult of the same species; for example, a caterpillar and a moth or butterfly

a.   From the Latin for "small active animal": *larval*

b.   Name given by Darwin as part of his theory of evolution

c.   From the Greek *larva, larua,* "a mask"

84.   **LAUDANUM**   Tincture of opium

a.   From the Latin *laudus,* "praiseworthy," as it relieved pain

b.   Word made up by Paracelsus to describe this mixture

c.   From a confusion with another drug of the time, the name of which sounded much the same

85. **LAVALIERE (sometimes lavalliere)**   Usually a jeweled pendant worn around the neck on a chain, sometimes a bow tied around the neck

   a. From the Old French word for throat, *la valle*

   b. The maker of the first such neck ornament was a jeweler who called his shop La Valiere

   c. From the duchesse de la Valliere (1644–1710), who popularized the style at the French court

86. **LEFT**   That side opposite to the hand normally favored by people (about ten to one); that side facing downstream; and so on

   a. From the Latin meaning "opposite"

   b. Source unknown, but many fanciful derivations

   c. From Old English "weak," via *lyftadl*, "paralysis"

87. **LEISURE**   Time free from employment; free from necessary business

   a. From the Old French *leisir*, derived from Latin *licere*, "to be permitted"

   b. A word invented by Milton to use in one of his poems describing the playful activities of the Greek gods and goddesses

   c. By back-formation from "lay" in the pronunciation of eighteenth-century England (*tea*, for example, was pronounced "tay")

88. **LIMOUSINE**   Large, closed motorcar, originally with a partition separating driver from passengers; often any large car

   a. From the inventor of such a vehicle, William J. Limousin of the Daimler-Benz motorcar company

   b. From the Latin *limen*, or "threshold," as it was necessary to step up and across the threshold of the original models, which did not have running boards

   c. From Limousin in France, where the first limousines were apparently made

89. **LINOLEUM** A floor covering made from a fabric that has been impregnated with a mixture of resins, fillers (usually cork), and oxidized linseed oil
    a. From F. Walton, who invented the process approximately 1859 and patented it
    b. From the Latin *linum*, "flax," and *oleum*, "oil"
    c. An invented name, made up by the first factory that produced it, but not trademarked or patented

90. **LOFT** Generally, an open space directly under the roof; an upper floor
    a. From Old German for "roof"
    b. From Old French for "attic" or "garret space"
    c. From Old English and German: *Luft*, "the air"

91. **LONGAN** A particular type of tree; its fruit, something like the lichi
    a. From Longan, in Asia Minor, where the tree originally grew and from which it was brought home by the Crusaders
    b. From the Chinese *lung yen*, "the Dragon's Eye"
    c. Arthur C. Longan produced the hybrid from a cross between a lichi and a peach in 1905

92. **LOOT** To plunder; slang, "money"
    a. Thieves' slang in London in the seventeenth century
    b. From Old English meaning "to borrow," hence not to return
    c. From the Hindi *lut*, "to plunder"

93. **LUDO** A board game in which counters are moved
    a. From Wilhelm Ludovicus, a monk who invented the game sometime during the Middle Ages (ca. 1300)
    b. From Old French, meaning "a war cry"—figuratively—indicating a win
    c. From the Latin *ludo*, "I play"

94. **LUTE** An old stringed instrument, made of wood, shaped like a pear cut in half down the middle
    a. Via the French, originally from the Arabic *al-'ud*, "the wood"
    b. Original completely unknown; it first appeared in an inventory taken at Henry VII's palace

   c. From the French *lutier,* "one who plays music"

95. **LUTETIA** The old name for Paris, France

   a. From the goddess Lutetia, who was alleged to have founded Paris

   b. After Lutetia in Italy, where the original settlers had lived

   c. From Latin *Lutetia Parisiorum,* "the mud town of the Parisii" (*lutum* means "mud" in Latin)

96. **LYNCH** To judge and put to death without benefit of a formal trial

   a. From the practice of hanging people from a nailed-up linchpin

   b. From a word invented by Shakespeare in one of his plays, indicating this sort of action

   c. From Captain William Lynch of Virginia

97. **MACABRE** Gruesome—like the Dance of Death

   a. Origin unknown or doubtful

   b. From the Hebrew *meqaber,* "a gravedigger"

   c. From the title of a painting by Hieronymus Bosch, showing a Danse Macabre, in which he apparently made up the term

98. **MACADAM** A smooth, hard road surface

   a. From the town in Scotland where the material was originally prepared

   b. From John Loudon McAdam (1756–1836), who invented it

   c. From the Scottish architect and road builder who worked on the estate of Lord McAdam, and who called it after his patron

99. **MACH** Usually "Mach number," the ratio of the air speed of an aircraft to the velocity of sound under particular conditions

   a. From the Greek *makina,* "machine"

   b. Short for machine speed

   c. From Ernst Mach, Austrian physicist (1838–1916)

100. **MAGENTA** A special tint of red with a purplish tinge

   a. From Julio Magenta, who discovered how to extract the dye in 1859

   b. Apparently in commemoration of the Battle of Magenta, in 1859, as it was discovered at that time

    c. From the Greek *magen, magentos,* "deep purple"

101. **MAGNET** The lodestone; anything with the properties of the lodestone, namely, attracting other objects, used figuratively of anything that attracts

    a. From the *magnetis lithos,* "Magnesian stone," from Magnesia, probably in Lydia

    b. An astronomer's term for the North Pole, when it was believed that the Pole attracted iron

    c. From the earliest form of compass, invented by an individual unknown except for his name, Magnetus

102. **MAGNOLIA** An Asiatic and American genus of trees with beautiful large solitary flowers and lovely foliage

    a. From Magnolus, in the Near East, where the trees first appeared

    b. From the Latin *magnus,* "great," referring to the size of the flowers

    c. From Pierre Magnol, a French botanist (1638–1715)

103. **MAILLOT** A one-piece, close-fitting bathing suit for women, sometimes ballet dancers' tights

    a. From the great ballerina Tatiana Maillot (1865–1905), who popularized the garment

    b. From the Italian, pronounced *mio,* and sometimes spelled that way, meaning "mine"

    c. From the French, meaning "swaddling clothes"

104. **MALAPROPISM** Misuse of words by misunderstanding, not by mispronunciation

    a. From Mrs. Malaprop, who misused words this way in Sheridan's play *The Rivals*

    b. From the French *mal apropos,* meaning "out of place" or "unsuitable"

    c. Both of the above, as Sheridan used the French expression for the name of his character

105. **MAMMON** Riches or the god of riches

    a. An ancient deity of Assyria

    b. Through medieval Latin from Greek *mamonas* or *mammonas,* originally Aramaic *mamon,* "riches"

c. From the Old Norse, meaning "money"

106. **MANGY** Having the mange, shabby, mean
   a. From the official name of the disease that afflicts dogs, *mangiosus canus*
   b. From the Latin *manducare*, "to chew," via the French, *mangé*, "eaten"
   c. Slang term originally, origin unknown

107. **MANSION** A large house, generally of some magnificence (common usage today, though formerly it meant other things, such as an apartment house, in England)
   a. From the Old English for a manor house, the home of a lord
   b. From Old French *mansione*, meaning "dwelling places"
   c. From Latin *manere*, "to remain"

108. **MAP** A representation in outline of the surface of a country, the moon, the Earth, a portion of any of these; to make a map of some place
   a. From the first book of maps, called *Mappa Mundi*
   b. From the Latin meaning "napkin" or "painted cloth," *mappa;* some evidence it was originally Punic
   c. From the same book as (a), except that the *Mappa* portion referred to the author

109. **MAQUIS** A thick cluster of shrubs, particularly in Corsica and along the Mediterranean shores; since World War II, a member of the French resistance forces, or the forces themselves
   a. From the Latin *macula*, "mesh," through Italian and French
   b. From the original name of the shrub in the early Corsican dialect: *macqui*
   c. From an older, unidentified word meaning "fighter," as the shrubs are thorny and offer much resistance

110. **MARASCHINO** A cherry preserved in maraschino, a liqueur made in Dalmatia; the liqueur itself
   a. The town in Dalmatia where the cherries were first grown, the name then being applied to all liqueurs and cherries of the same type

b. From the name of the man, Johannes Marashk, whose family business first made the liqueur under his supervision in 1586

c. From Italian *marasca*, or *amarasca*, "a sour cherry," from the Latin *amarus*, "bitter"

111. **MARKET**   A place where goods are sold; to sell goods or services; a building, square, or other public place used for such purposes

a. From Germanic *Mark*, a unit of money, representing a place where money or services were bought or traded

b. From Latin *mercator*, "a trade," via *merx*, "merchandise"

c. From the same root as *marker*, because the market was once a strictly delineated space where buying and selling could occur; it was against the law to sell merchandise elsewhere, as this way tax records could be kept

112. **MARMALADE**   A jam or preserve generally made of the rind and pulp of bitter oranges—sometimes sweet, but more often of the bitter type

a. When Mary, Queen of Scots, was ill, this was the only food she would eat, hence it was called "Marie Malade" (sick Mary)

b. Via the French, through Portuguese, *marmelada*, "a quince," originally from Latin *melimelon*, "a honey apple"

c. From the Old English meaning "to cook fruit"

113. **MAROON**   A brownish crimson color

a. From Italian *marrone* and French *marron*, meaning "chestnut"

b. From the painter Pietro Marrone, of the Early Italian school (ca. 1410), who used this color a great deal

c. From the Latin word *maron*, for "brown earth"

114. **MARSHAL**   An officer in a royal household, formerly in charge of the horses; as a verb, to draw up in order; in the United States (but not England) the head of a police or fire company, or similar official

a. From *marscal*, "a leader," Arabic, a word picked up at the time of the Crusades

b. From *mare,* Latin for "a female horse," and *scalla,* "leader of the troupe"

c. From Old French *mareschal,* from Old High German *Marah,* "a horse," and *schall,* "one who serves"

115. **MARTINET** A strict disciplinarian; someone who is unreasonably strict; a naval or military officer who is unnecessarily harsh with the men under his command

a. From the Roman god of war, Mars, who was the patron of fierce soldiers

b. From General Martinet, who became known for the strict code of drill rules he drew up for Louis XIV of France

c. From Martin of Tours, the famous French soldier who fought against the Moors—"martinet" being the diminutive of Martin

116. **MASOCHISM** Gratification obtained from suffering

a. From the Greek *masoch,* "to suffer"

b. From the writer Sacher-Masoch, who described this condition

c. From a play called (in translation) *The Masochist,* by Molière

117. **MATADOR** In bullfights, the person who does the actual killing

a. Via Spanish *matador,* derived from the verb *matar,* "to kill," from Latin *mactare,* one meaning of which is "to kill for a sacrificial honor," from *mactus,* "honored"

b. From Bizet's opera *Carmen,* in which he erroneously used the term instead of picador, the person who places the picks, and from there erroneously adopted

c. From the Greek for "bull," *maura,* and then via the Romans to Spain

118. **MATRICULATE** To be enrolled as a member, especially of a college or university or series of lectures, and so on

a. From the original root for mother, *mater,* as colleges and universities are often called alma mater (dear mother)

b. From the diminutive of *matrix* in medieval Latin, *matricula*

c. From *matriculos,* meaning "a course of studies," medieval Latin

119. **MATTRESS** A pad for a bed, usually stuffed with hair and other materials; a foundation for a road
    a. From the Arabic *al-matrah,* meaning "a place where anything is thrown"
    b. Originally matellase, meaning "quilted," because individuals slept on quilted pads
    c. Originally an engineering term, as people normally slept on the floor, and then the term for underpadding was adopted for sleeping arrangements

120. **MAUSOLEUM** A magnificent tomb or a splendid monument in honor of a deceased person
    a. From the Greek for tomb, *mausol*
    b. From the Latin *mausoleum,* meaning "a tomb that shows respect"
    c. From the exceptionally grand tomb at Halicarnassus, built by the widow of one Mausolos (died ca. 353 B.C.)

121. **MAYDAY** The international distress signal for watercraft and airborne traffic via radio-telephone
    a. From the early days of telegraph, because the Morse-code signal is extremely easy to send
    b. Linguists picked the two easiest sounds to hear and identify, and they were universally adopted
    c. From the French *m'aidez,* "help me"—pronounced "mayday"

122. **MEANDER** To wander, to follow a winding or obscure path; as a noun, a wandering walk or route
    a. From Greek Maiandros, a very winding river in Asia Minor, through Latin *meander*
    b. Derived from Old English words for "mead" and "wander," implying the path taken by someone drunk on mead
    c. Origin unknown, first appeared in a Spenserian poem, perhaps as a neologism

123. **MEERSCHAUM** A fine, light clay; the pipe made from this type of clay
    a. The clay was first worked in Mereskaum in Holland, and took its name from that place

b. The clay was originally thought to be petrified sea-foam, German *Meer*, "sea" and *Schaum*, "foam" or "scum"

c. Originally sold in the shop of Johannes Meerschaum in London in the eighteenth century (ca. 1756)

124. **MELANCHOLY** Dejection, melancholia, deep sadness

   a. From the Greek ruler Melanchthon, who was noted for his deep moods of depression

   b. From the Greek *melancholia*, combining *melas* and *chole*, meaning "black bile"

   c. The Romans, who had a presiding spirit for everything, had a goddess called Melancholia, who looked after depressed individuals

125. **MENACE** To threaten danger, to act in a manner so as to suggest danger; as a noun, someone or something that is a danger

   a. From the Old English for *maen*, "man," and *aex*, "axe"; literally, "the man with the axe"

   b. From the Latin, via French, but originally *minae*, "overhanging parts" (plural *minaciae*)

   c. From the executioner of Louis XIV, M. Menarce, who was a prominent figure of the time

126. **MENTOR** An adviser, usually a wise one; a tutor; a helpful, wise counselor

   a. From the Latin *mentor, mentorus*, "of wise mind"

   b. From Mentor, the guiding spirit of Telemachus, in Greek legend

   c. From Old German, a corruption of the word meaning "the king's assistant"

127. **MESMERIZE** Usually used rather loosely as to fascinate, dominate, or fix the attention of; actually to put into a state of light hypnosis

   a. From Friedrich or Franz Anton Mesmer (ca. 1775), a German doctor who demonstrated the powers of hypnosis

   b. From the Old English form of *mzed*, "mind," hence *maezmer*

c. From the first apparatus, a swinging pendulum used for hypnosis, made in the workshop of a glassmaker named Mesmer

128. **METICULOUS** Extremely   careful,   scrupulous,   perhaps overly careful

a. From the Greek for "web" or "mesh," *metis, meticulous,* in that such a person lets nothing slip through the mesh

b. From the Latin, *meticulosus,* "frightened"

c. Derived from Latin, through early French, via Middle English, from *meticulum,* meaning "an overseer"

129. **MIGRAINE**   A condition marked by recurring headaches, often one-sided

a. From Dr. Antoine Migraine (ca. 1315), who first described the condition

b. From the Latin word for salt, *granum,* as the condition was believed to be caused by excess salt in the body

c. From the French, through the Greek *hemikrania: hemi,* "half," plus *kranion,* "skull"

130. **MILE**   Now, an American measurement of 5,280 feet, in Great Britain, approximately 1.61 km statute miles

a. From the Latin *milia,* plural of *mille,* "one thousand" (paces was implied)

b. From Old English *maele,* a unit of time measuring about twenty minutes, the walking time for a mile

c. From Old English *meal,* "milepost," marking off distances

131. **MILLINER**   A maker and/or seller of women's hats, headgear, and trimmings

a. Via the French *miliniere,* meaning "decorations," from Old French, probably *miriane*

b. From Mme. Millinère, who first opened a shop in Paris to sell hats; previously, hats for ladies had been privately made

c. From *Milaner,* someone who traded in goods from Milan, particularly decorative ribbons and the like used in trimming hats for ladies

132. **MINIATURE** Now, commonly, a painting on a very small scale; anything reduced in size

    a. From the Italian *miniatura,* Latin *minium,* meaning "red lead," used for manuscript illumination (meaning changed by association with *mini,* "small")

    b. From the obvious meaning of the Latin *mini,* meaning "small"

    c. From the famous painter of tiny portraits on ivory, G. Miniaturae, who developed (ca. 1650) this special form of portraiture for necklace pendants

133. **MISERICORD** Now, usually, a bracket on a turn-up seat on a permanent pew in church choir or other location

    a. From Latin *miserere,* meaning "to suffer," popular slang of the time for sitting, standing, or kneeling in a cold, drafty church for a long time

    b. From the Latin for *misericordia,* "tender hearted," for it allowed the aged or infirm some measure of rest during services

    c. These wooden objects are all carved and had to be executed while the carver was lying on his back on the hard stone floor, hence they were called "miserables"

134. **MNEMONIC** A device to help the memory, such as the rhyme "Thirty days hath September"

    a. The Greek word for "memory," *mnemo,* plus *syne,* "to make easy"

    b. From the initials of the first word of a verse designed to teach a Bible chapter

    c. From Mnemosyne, one of the Titans, who was the mother of the Muses in Greek mythology

135. **MOB** A disorderly crowd, the rabble, a gang; to behave like a group, to attack as a group of unruly individuals

    a. From the Latin *mobile vulgus,* "the fickle (or changeable) multitude"

    b. From the initials in "*Men of Blood,*" from bands of ruffians who roamed the streets before the police force was founded in London

    c. From the Old English *moeb,* meaning "to assemble unlawfully"

136. **MOHOLE** A hole drilled through the Earth's crust and into the mantle
    a. From "*m*iddle *o*f (the Earth) *hole*"
    b. From the machine used to drill the hole, which is of enormous length, *m*otorized *hole* digger
    c. From Andrija Mohorovičić, of Croatia, who developed the theory that the Earth is composed of layers

137. **MONEY** Coins, units of exchange, pieces of metal indicating a value stamped thereon, anything used as a medium for commercial transactions
    a. From the French *monnaie,* meaning "medium of exchange"
    b. From Assyrian, the earliest coins having the likeness of King Monius stamped on them
    c. From the Latin (through several changes) from *moneta,* "money" or "mint," as money was coined in the temple of Juno Moneta

138. **MORPHINE** Another name for morphia, the major alkaloid in the hypnotic drug opium
    a. From the Latin name for the alkaloid, *morphitus,* as it was discovered during Roman times
    b. From Paul Morphia, the chemist (ca. 1810) who first developed the purified form of the product
    c. From the Greek god of sleep, Morpheus

139. **MORTGAGE** To sign or pledge as security for a debt; a conditional transfer to be canceled upon payment of an obligation
    a. From the medieval Latin *morgage,* "debt"
    b. From the Norse *mord,* "owing," plus *gagne,* "money"
    c. Old French *mort,* "dead," and *gage,* "a pledge"

140. **MUSCLE** The tissue forming a contractile structure by which movement of the body is effected
    a. From Latin *musculus,* "a muscle, a mouse"
    b. From the Old French *muscleiller,* "to contract"
    c. From the Norse *muskelum,* "to perspire"

141. **MUSTARD** The genus *Brassica;* the condiment made from plants in this genus, usually quite pungent
    a. From the French *moutarde,* named for the cook of Louis XIII who invented this special delicacy for the king
    b. From the Latin *mustum,* meaning "new wine," with which the condiment was always made
    c. From an unknown source, possibly Arabic *al-matar,* "the spicy thing"

142. **NADIR** The lowest point of anything; the position exactly opposite the zenith
    a. From Latin *nadum,* "the depths"
    b. From the Greek word for the underworld, *nadirus,* representing the lowest possible point
    c. From the Arabic *nazir* or *nadir,* "opposite to"

143. **NARCISSUS** Daffodil, from the Amaryllis family
    a. Name given by Linnaeus when he set up his classification system for plants
    b. From the city of Narcissa, in Greece, where the plants were first cultivated
    c. From Narcissus, a Greek youth who fell in love with his own reflection in a pool, did nothing but look at himself, and was changed into the flower

144. **NASTURTIUM** A garden flower, a form of cress
    a. Named for James Naster, British gardener (1810–1898), who hybridized it into today's flower
    b. From the Greek *nastertia,* meaning "cress"
    c. From the Latin *nasus,* "nose," and *torquere,* "to twist," because of its very strong odor, which is displeasing to many

145. **NAUSEA** A strong inclination to vomit, a feeling of extreme malaise
    a. From Old Norse, meaning "sickening," *knowsa*
    b. A corruption of an Old English word now lost, meaning "disgusting"
    c. Through Latin from Greek *naus,* "a ship," to *nausia,* "seasickness"

146. **NEIGHBOR**   A person or thing close by—neighboring field, for one close by, a neighbor for a person living close by
    a.   From the Old English *neight,* "bleating" or "braying," hence anyone or anything within reach of this sound
    b.   Old English *neah,* "near," plus *gebur,* "farmer"
    c.   An invented word from Chaucer, who used it for the first time in the *Canterbury Tales*

147. **NEON**   Atomic number 10, a gas found in the atmosphere
    a.   Discovered by Sir William Neon (1852–1916)
    b.   Discovered by Sir William Ramsey (1852–1916) and named from the Greek *neos,* "new"
    c.   From the Roman goddess of light, *Neona*

148. **NEWS**   Reports of recent events, material for inclusion in newspapers
    a.   From Middle English *newes,* untraceable earlier
    b.   From the initials of *N*orth, *S*outh, *E*ast, and *W*est, arranged to form "NEWS"
    c.   The plural of *new,* from the Greek *neos*

149. **NICKEL**   A metal, white, magnetic, atomic number 28; a U.S. coin worth five cents made of this material
    a.   From the Spanish word for "small coin," now extinct, *nicola*
    b.   From Nickelaus, in Germany, where the metal was first found
    c.   From German *Kupfer-Nickel,* composed of *Kupfer,* "copper," and *Nickel,* "a small goblin," because the ore looked just like copper but was not, perhaps because of the activities of the little demon

150. **NICOTINE**   A poisonous alkaloid derived from tobacco leaves
    a.   From Jean Nicot, who originally sent leaves of tobacco to Catherine de Medicis, in France, who named the product after him
    b.   From Nicotiana, a town in Cyprus, where the tobacco plant was first naturalized and domesticated in Europe
    c.   From the Greek for "stupefying plant," *nicotia*

151. **NOON**   Now, midday
   a. Originally, the ninth hour in Latin and in church services (nones); but when the nones services were shifted to midday, nones became noon
   b. From the expression in Middle English, *height noon*, or high noon; the time when the sun was at its zenith
   c. From the Old German *Knoen*, "the midday meal"

152. **OCEAN**   The saltwater covering that encircles the globe and consists of most of the Earth's covering; any of its divisions, such as the Atlantic Ocean
   a. From the Greek Okeanos, the river that is supposed to encircle the Earth, personified by the god of the same name
   b. The early Hebrew for the word meaning last waters, *oshana*
   c. Egyptian derivation, from the original Egyptian word for the Nile, Okanas, "father of waters"

153. **ORIENT**   The place where the sun rises; the Far East, for Europeans and Americans
   a. From the Aramaic *orens*, meaning "eastern"
   b. From Arabic *al-orient*, the direction toward which prayers should be made
   c. From the Latin, past participle of *oriri*, "to rise"

154. **OUNCE**   A measure of weight
   a. From the Old English *oz*, a measure of weight for grains of wheat
   b. From the Latin *oz*, meaning "to measure in small quantities"
   c. From Latin *uncia*, "a twelfth part," as it was once the twelfth part of a troy pound, which is now generally obsolete, except in certain instances

155. **OXYGEN**   A gas (atomic number 8), which supports both life and combustion; colorless, tasteless, and odorless
   a. From the Latin root *oxy*, meaning "composed of eight atoms"
   b. A coined word, made up by J. B. Priestley, who was investigating its properties

    c. From the Greek word root *oxy*, "sharp," and a derivation of *gennain*, meaning "to originate" or "generate," as the Greeks thought all acids included oxygen as a component

156. **PALACE** The residence of a ruler; a large and imposing residence of an official (sometimes, especially in England, a place of entertainment)

    a. From the Greek derivative of Pallas Athena, the queen of the goddesses, and hence her residence

    b. From Andrea Palladio, the Italian architect (1508–1580) and developer of the Palladian style of building

    c. From Latin *palatium*, from the emperor's custom of living on the Palatine Hill in Rome

157. **PAPER** Generally used to mean material that is made or manufactured for writing, wrapping, and similar purposes; a written or printed document

    a. Through Old French *papier*, via Latin *papyrus*, from the Greek *papyros*, "papyrus," from the paper reed of Egypt

    b. From *pap*, Old English, "a soft substance," eventually extended in meaning to both food and the pulp from which paper is made

    c. From Papeirein, the original name of the town in Germany where today's type of paper was first made

158. **PARAFFIN** Originally paraffin wax, discovered by Karl Reichenbach, a largely saturated hydrocarbon of the methane series

    a. Named by the discoverer for his daughter, Parafine—the finest

    b. Named by the discoverer because of its poor affinity for other compounds due to its high saturation: Latin *parum*, "little," plus *affinis*, "having affinity"

    c. From the name of the building where the laboratory was situated, Parafinnus Hall

159. **PARAPHERNALIA** Items of ornament and accessories, trappings, equipment, and the like

    a. From a made-up word, coined by Spenser in the *Faerie Queene*, to describe material and trappings the queen brought with her

    b. From the French, meaning "useless ornamentation," the original word being *parapherie*

    c. From Greek, through Latin, being originally *para*, "beyond," and *pherne*, "a bride's dowry," and representing the possessions a woman kept in her own name after marriage

160. **PEDAGOGUE** A teacher, one who instructs, often used in a pejorative sense

    a. From the Middle Latin *paedo*, a combined form meaning "children" (as in pediatrician)

    b. From Greek, the name of Sophocles' tutor, Paedagogus

    c. Via Latin, from the Greek *paidagogos*, a servant who led a boy—walking, naturally—to his lessons, from the root words meaning "boy" and "lead"

161. **PEN** A writing instrument, especially one using ink, as a noun; to write, as a verb

    a. From the Latin *penna*, meaning "a feather"

    b. From a Middle English abbreviation of an unknown Saxon word meaning "writing instrument"; original word lost

    c. A neologism first used by Chaucer in one of his stories to avoid using a foreign word

162. **PERSON** A sentient being, a human being, an individual; the human figure

    a. From the Aramaic for "shape," *peirson*

    b. From the Latin *persona*, "a mask," worn by actors

    c. Origin unknown, apparently common to many early languages

163. **PLIMSOLL LINE** A mark on the side of a ship showing the load lines for different waters and different conditions, as required by law

    a. From *plimsoll*, a deck shoe worn by sailors who went down the side of the ship to paint the lines

    b. From Samuel Plimsoll (1824–1898), who got the law passed in England

    c. From *plumb*, Latin for "even" or "straight hanging," and *solus*, "solution" (in other words, that the ship would be even in the water)

164. **POINSETTIA** A spurge with colored leaves that look like flowers in petallike bracts
    a. From Poinsett, in England, the garden where the plant was first developed in the greenhouse
    b. From the famous Poinsett gardens in Gibraltar, which specialized in semitropical plants
    c. From Joel Roberts Poinsett (1779–1851), the American minister to Mexico, who imported it

165. **POLITE** Courteous, adhering to the standards of generally accepted behavior
    a. A back-formation from "political," originally used in a satirical manner
    b. From the Greek word *pol,* meaning "people"
    c. From Latin *politus,* the past participle of "polish"

166. **POPLIN** A woven fabric with a warp and weft (woof) of different materials; a similar weave of all cotton or some other thread, woven to give that effect
    a. From *populus,* "(cloth) of the people," and linen (which was cloth for aristocrats)
    b. From *pauwpeline,* meaning "mixed weave" in early French
    c. Possibly from *papeline,* as it was made in Avignon during the time the popes resided there

167. **PORPOISE** A member of the dolphin family with a short snout, averaging four to eight feet in length
    a. From the Old English *por,* "to do," and *pose,* "place," as the dolphin frequently placed itself out of the water, not like the fish it resembles
    b. From Latin *porcus,* "a hog," plus Latin *piscis,* "a fish," for the alleged resemblance
    c. Porposa was a Greek deity of the sea who sometimes appeared in this form

168. **PRALINE** A form of sweet candy made with crushed nuts, or a nut kernel, coated with (usually) melted brown sugar
    a. From the Old French for roasted brown sugar, *pralinée*
    b. From the confectionery shop in New Orleans, on Praline Street, where these confections were first sold

    c. From the marshal Duplessis-Praslin, whose cook invented the delicacy for the French court

169. **PRECOCIOUS** Reaching a particular stage of development earlier than the norm: often applied to children showing early mental maturity

    a. From the same source as dementia praecox, a form of insanity—"early ripe, early rot"

    b. From *praekos*, Greek, meaning "a gifted child"

    c. From the Latin *praecox*, "to cook" or "ripen"

170. **PREJUDICE** Predisposition in favor of or, usually, against something without sufficient knowledge; an opinion formed without due examination, or developed in advance

    a. From the French *préjudice*, "wrong," and the Latin word *judicium*, "judgment"

    b. From the Latin *judice*, meaning "to pass sentence on a convicted criminal"

    c. From the French *pré-*, "before," and *judice*, "opinion"

171. **PREVARICATE** To evade the truth; to shift from side to side; to betray a client by colluding with his opponent (British legal)

    a. From the Latin *prevaricari*, "to walk crookedly"

    b. From the Latin *pre*, meaning "before," and a misreading of *varus* for *verus*, "the truth"

    c. From the Old English *prevolix*, "a liar"

172. **PROFILE** A portrait, usually a head, in side view; the side face; an outline; to shape the outline of

    a. Via Italian *profilo*, from the Latin *pro*, "before," and *filo*, "a thread"

    b. From Johannus Profilum, the medieval artist who first drew this type of outline picture (fl. 1350)

    c. From the Egyptian: a description of the usual form of drawing a human face, in profile

173. **PTOMAINE** A name for amino compounds, now usually used loosely, formed from decaying animal matter, sometimes poisonous

    a. From Ptolemy, the Egyptian king, whose mummy was the first one found

b. From the Greek word *ptoma,* "a corpse"

c. A misprint in the early textbooks of medicine, in which *st* was misread as *pt;* so the word should have been *stomaine,* "stomach poisoning"

174. **PUCK (or POOK)** A mischievous spirit; a sprite

a. Word invented by Rudyard Kipling for his book *Puck of Pook's Hill*

b. From Old Norse *puki,* Welsh and Old English *puca*

c. From "puck," the disk used instead of a ball in (ice) hockey, and the way it slides and flies around

175. **PUNCH** An alcoholic mix, traditionally consisting of alcohol in some form, water, sugar, lemon juice, and spices—numerous variations exist

a. From the strength of the drink, which delivers a real "punch"

b. From the Hindi word for "five," *pac,* possibly Sanskrit *paci*

c. From the type of bowl in which it was served—usually a silver bowl with "punched" designs in its rim

176. **PUPIL (1)** A student, one who is being taught; special meanings in law

a. From the diminutives of *pupus,* "boy," and *pupa,* "girl," in Latin

b. From Catlinus Pupillus, a famous teacher in the age of Julius Caesar

c. From the Old Norse *puppa,* "puppy"

177. **PUPIL (2)** The round opening in the eye through which light passes; used figuratively for other openings of the same sort

a. From the Latin *pupila,* meaning "an aperture"

b. From the Latin for "boy," *pupus,* and "girl," *pupa,* referring to the small size of the images in the eye, a diminutive

c. From a misreading of early medical texts; we do not know exactly what this portion of the eye was called by early physicians

178. **PUPPET** A marionette, a doll moved by wires or strings; one who acts under the advice of others, as if pulled by strings

a. From *poppet,* a term of endearment for a young, naïve girl in Shakespeare's plays

b. From the Latin *pupa,* "girl," diminutive

c. From Old French *poupette,* a word made up by Racine

179. **PUPPY**   A young dog; an immature man; a rude young man

a. From the Latin, a diminutive of *pupa*

b. From Old German *Poep,* "a small dog"

c. Origin unknown

180. **PYREX (TM)**   A type of glass that is resistant to fire (trademarked)

a. From the name of the manufacturer, Mr. Pyrum

b. From the town in which this glass was first made, Pyros, in Greece

c. From the Greek *pyr,* meaning "fire," and *rex,* meaning "king"

181. **QUARANTINE**   Isolation or detention, usually compulsory, for persons, animals, or ships under suspicion of carrying infectious disease

a. The section of the old ports of Europe where ships were quarantined was known as the *quaranta,* being forty paces from the nearest person

b. From the Old English for "contagious," *knorant*

c. From the forty-day period originally used for such isolation

182. **QUICK**   Fast, swift, speedy, alive (as in "the quick and the dead")

a. From Old English *cwic,* derived from Old Norse *kvikr,* "living" or "alive"

b. From the Greek for "speed," *kikos*

c. From Old English *kweykr,* "to bloom early"

183. **RAW**   Uncooked, in a natural state, not prepared

a. From the Latin *rara,* "rare"

b. From the sound, as "raw" was believed to sound like tearing meat apart or an animal's roar

c. From Old English *hreaw,* meaning "uncooked"

184. **REEF**   A shoal or bank; rocks lying near the surface of the water, especially the sea

a. From the Phoenician *raefos,* "rock-rimmed"

b. Origin unknown; many speculative derivations

c. From Old Norse *rif,* "reef"

185. **REHEARSE**   To say over, to repeat lines (especially of a play or other performance); to play music over and over in preparation for a performance
    a.   From Latin *re,* "again," and *harse,* "to play at"
    b.   From the French *rehearser,* "to sing again"
    c.   From the Latin, through Old French, for *re,* "again," and *hirpex,* "a rake" or "harrow"

186. **RELENT**   To become less severe
    a.   From *re,* "again," and *lentos,* "moving slowly," in Old Latin
    b.   From *relentarius,* "pliant" or "yielding," in Latin
    c.   From Latin *re,* "back," and *lentus,* "sticky" or "sluggish"

187. **REMORSE**   Conscience, as demonstrated by the pain felt
    a.   From *remordere,* the Latin for "to bite again"
    b.   Via Old English, from the Norse word for conscience, *kremordun*
    c.   Of unknown origin, dating back to Middle English, when it appeared in several writings simultaneously

188. **RHAPSODY**   A piece of music of irregular form; intense ecstatic feeling
    a.   From the Greek goddess of music, Rhapsos
    b.   From the Greek, originally *rhaptein,* "to sew," and *oide,* "a song"
    c.   From the title of one of Milton's poems called "A Rhapsody," which was set to music, and the name came to be attached to anything similar

189. **RIALTO**   A raised bridge; also a district in Venice, mentioned in Shakespeare, and often used as a generic term for a busy or business district
    a.   From Giuseppe Rialto, a famous jeweler who put up money to build the bridge on which he put his shop
    b.   From the Rialto family, famous bankers of Venice
    c.   A contraction of Italian *rialzato,* meaning "raised," like a bridge

190. **RIBBON**   A narrow band or strip; or anything else, such as a road stripe, that has a similar form
    a.   From the Latin *ribandus,* meaning "a narrow strip of cloth"

    b. From the Old French *robonne,* from the town in southern France where the narrow ribbon looms were first developed

    c. From the Old French, origin unknown or obscure

191. **RITZY** Ostentatiously rich or showy (from the Ritz chain of hotels)

    a. The hotel chain used the word "Ritz" to suggest rich without actually saying it

    b. The word *ritz* is an Old English form of "rich" and predated the hotels

    c. The Ritz hotels were named after Caesar Ritz, a famous hotelier who opened the first one

192. **ROBE** A form of clothing, usually a loose gown or outer covering, often used for evening wear

    a. From the Latin *robus,* a clergyman's ritual loose cloak

    b. From the Old French *robe,* originally "plunder" or "booty" (as in rob)

    c. From the Middle English *hroeb,* meaning "fancy cloth"

193. **RODENT** Mammals such as squirrels, rats, rabbits, and beavers who have no canine teeth and prominent incisors

    a. Old English *rodentus,* the word for a type of northern European squirrel

    b. From the Latin *rodere,* "to gnaw"

    c. From the original German version of the Pied Piper of Hamelin in which the leader of the rats was called Rodentus

194. **ROOK** A chess piece now in the form of a castle

    a. Originally birdlike in shape, named for the European rook, a type of crow

    b. From *rookh,* the Middle English word for the location of a fortified hilltop

    c. From the Persian *rukh,* "a castle"

195. **ROSTER** A list of names showing the order of appearance for duty; the duties assigned

    a. From the Latin *rostere,* "to call out" or "count"

    b. From the Dutch *rooster,* "gridiron"

    c.   From the official title of the officer assigned to make up daily duty lists in the British Army

196. **ROUÉ** A dissolute person, a gambler, a rake

    a.   From the French, meaning "to gamble"

    b.   From the French, after a friend of Prince Philippe, duc d'Orléans (ca. 1715), who coined the word

    c.   From the French *rouer,* "to break on the wheel," a form of torture

197. **RUBRIC** A heading, a direction, a guiding principle

    a.   From Latin *rubrica,* "red ocher," as the rules were underlined or written in red

    b.   From the Old German *Hrubrick,* "a governing body"

    c.   From French *rubrice,* meaning "an obscure law"

198. **SABOTAGE** Any underhanded or secret action taken to prevent the completion of a task; usually industrial or military

    a.   From General Sabote (1796–1845), who acted for Napoleon and against the British by setting up a force of "saboteurs" after the British victory at Waterloo

    b.   From *sabot,* a wooden shoe worn by French peasants and workers who showed great initiative in slowing down projects they did not wish to see completed

    c.   Origin unknown—probably the name of a resistance fighter in World War I

199. **SALARY** Payment for services; wages, but usually not for day labor

    a.   From *sala,* Arabic for "seven," as wages were paid every seventh day

    b.   Old English *hsaelar,* the money coin usually paid to soldiers

    c.   From the Latin *salarium,* "salt money"

200. **SALMON** A highly prized fish that ascends rivers to spawn; there are a number of related species and types

    a.   From its color, salmon, a pinkish red

    b.   From the Latin *salmo, salmonis,* from *salire,* "to leap"

    c.   From the river in Iceland where they were first observed moving upstream to spawn

201. **SARCASM** A jibe; a satirical or sneering remark; a cutting saying
   a. From Sarcasus, a character in an early Greek play who specialized in such language
   b. Origin generally unknown
   c. From the Greek, originally, with the root word *sarkasmos*, "to tear flesh like dogs"

202. **SATURN** The Roman god of agriculture, usually identified with the Greek god Kronos; one of the major planets
   a. From the name of the holiday, Saturnalia, celebrated at the time this planet is most clearly visible in the sky
   b. From the Latin *serrere*, "to sow," from the function attributed to this god
   c. From the Latin word for melancholy, *saturnus*, meaning "melancholy," from which we get "saturnine"

203. **SAXIFRAGE** A plant of the "London Pride" family
   a. From the Greek, through the Latin *saxumt*, "a stone," and *fragere*, "to break," because Pliny described it as good for breaking up calculus (stones) in the bladder
   b. From *saxon*, because the early Saxons grew the plant, and the Normans called it by the name of the local inhabitants
   c. A corruption of "sassafras," which it closely resembles; or vice-versa, sassafras being a corruption of saxifrage

204. **SCANDAL** Anything that brings discredit to fame or reputation
   a. From a word coined by Richard Brinsley Sheridan, when he wrote *School for Scandal*
   b. From Latin *scandalum*, taken from the almost identical Greek word, meaning "a stumbling block"
   c. From *escandol*, Spanish for "malicious gossip"

205. **SCATTER** To disperse widely by tossing loosely, or by other means; often used figuratively
   a. From Old English, first recorded instance seems to be the *Anglo-Saxon Chronicle* (for the year 1137), origin unknown
   b. From the American Indian word *skatch*, meaning "to sow seed corn" (with a scattering motion)
   c. From the French *scatterer*, meaning "to sprinkle"

206. **SCHEDULE**   A list, inventory, or table; a supplement; a form to be completed, or already completed, for filling in details

   a. From the Old English *hskedul,* "hour," indicating the time things were to be done

   b. From the Greek *skede,* through Latin to Old French *cedule,* with the original meaning "a strip of papyrus"

   c. From the British Army, origin unknown, perhaps Army slang

207. **SCRUTINY**   Extremely careful examination, close observance

   a. From the Latin *scrutinium* and *scrutari,* meaning "to search through the rags," that is, right to the bottom of a pile; from the word meaning "to search" and *scruta,* meaning "rags" or "trash"

   b. From the group of Norse languages, *skruat* and its equivalents, meaning "to examine with the eye of an eagle, or a sea bird" (*skrua*)

   c. Origin unknown

208. **SEA**   The ocean, the mass of saltwater that covers much of the Earth

   a. From the Phoenician, to the Greek, and then to Latin, *sea* meaning vast "waters"

   b. From Old Norse, Danish, and so on, *saer* and *sae*

   c. From the Egyptian word for "large lake," *sea,* as they did not have the basic idea of oceans

209. **SEARCH**   To examine; to seek out; to look for

   a. From Old English *hseark,* meaning "to look"

   b. From the Latin, originally *circare,* "to go about" (in a circle, *circus*)

   c. From the Scottish *sirk,* a legal process of search and seizure

210. **SECURE**   Safe, without danger, fixed in opinion

   a. From the Latin *se,* meaning "without," and *cara,* "care"

   b. From a prison that existed in Italy in the twelfth century, called the Secura, from which no one ever escaped

   c. From a special lock invented by G. Securus (fl. A.D. 1200), which was considered, at that time, to be foolproof

211. **SELTZER**   A mineral water, usually gasified

   a. From Nieder Selters in Prussia, the source of such water

b. From Johannes Seltzer, who invented an inexpensive way of carbonating water in 1790

c. From the first company to mass produce and sell sparkling water in sealed containers, owned by the Seltzer family of Brooklyn, New York, in the 1870s

212. **SENATE** A governing body; when capitalized, originally the ruling assembly of Rome; now used in the United States for the upper house of the legislative branch

a. The original Roman Senate met on the Senatus Hill, one of the seven hills of Rome

b. From the Latin for "old man," *senex senectatis*

c. From the Greek *senyx*, "assembly of wise ones"

213. **SERENADE** A musical piece, typically one sung to a particular person, usually performed at a lady's window; a composition something like a symphony, but less serious

a. From the Latin *serenus*, "bright, clear sky," and from there into French and Italian

b. From the title of a musical composition written in 1680 and called "Serenade" by an unknown court musician

c. From Serenus, one of Cupid's servants, who often played music for Cupid and his lady loves

214. **SHAKE** To disturb the balance or equilibrium of; to move with short, quick motions

a. Old English *sceacan*, meaning "to shake"

b. Latin, from *sacare*, "to thrust violently"

c. Derivation unknown; first appeared in Spenser's *Faerie Queen*

215. **SHAMROCK** A trifoliate plant, popularly called the lesser yellow trefoil; the national emblem of Ireland

a. From Irish *seamrog*, Gaelic *seamrag*, a diminutive of *seamar*, "the trefoil"

b. The emblem carried by the shamrock, a Gaelic sprite or wood fairy

c. From *shimrock*, as the plant was first observed growing in the crevices of rocks

216. **SHOP** A place where merchandise is sold, a store

a. From the Old English *schaepen*, "to buy"

b. From the Old English *sceoppa,* "a treasury"

c. From the Latin *sopa,* the area under the extended roof of the buildings of the Forum, where goods were sold

217. **SHRAPNEL**   A shell with a bursting explosive charge that is filled with musket balls; now any explosive shell filled with small shot of some sort

a. From General Shrapnel (1761–1842), who invented this form of shell

b. From Shrapenelle, in France, location of the first factory in France where these shells were made

c. From *schrappnel,* Old German, meaning "to strike multiple blows"

218. **SHUTTLE**   The apparatus that carries the threads of the weft between the threads of the warp in weaving

a. From the inventor, Alyssa Shuttle, English, ca. 1540–1595, who developed the modern-day shuttle from earlier, more primitive apparatus

b. From Old English *scytel,* "an arrow" or "dart," via *sceotan,* "to shoot"

c. Source unknown, because warp-and-weft weaving is so old it is impossible to determine exactly where the term originated

219. **SIESTA**   A nap, usually after lunch

a. From the town of Siesta in Spain, which local folklore claimed was the sleepiest town in the country

b. From the Latin *siestare,* "to nap"

c. From the Latin *sexta* (*hora,* or "hour," implied)

220. **SILHOUETTE**   An outline, normally a profile, of a shadow, traced and filled in with black or cut out of black paper

a. From *silhouettée,* French, meaning "outlined" or "traced"

b. From Latin *siler,* "to trace," plus *-ette,* a French diminutive, added later when these drawings became popular

c. From Étienne de Silhouette (1709–1767), though the reason the name has been attached to this type of drawing is not clear

221. **SIRLOIN** The upper part of a loin of beef, a specific cut, which differs in England and the United States
   a. Queen Elizabeth was so pleased with the beef she was served—this cut—that she said, "It shall be called Sir Loin"
   b. From the French *sur*, "over," and *longe*, "loin"
   c. From a case of mistaken identity involving the exact location of this cut of meat

222. **SLAVE** A person who is held as chattel or property
   a. From the Latin *slavere*, meaning "to serve"
   b. From unknown sources, possibly a made-up word used by early translators of the Bible
   c. From *Slav*, through *esclave*, in French, apparently because early slave labor came from conquered peoples of the Slavic regions

223. **SOAR** To climb—in the air, to a great height—to rise through the air (implication of easiness)
   a. From the Latin *ex*, "from," and *aura*, "air"
   b. A corruption of the name Icarus, the legendary figure who soared toward the sun and was killed
   c. From the Old German *schoor*, meaning "to fly"

224. **SOLDIER** A member of the military forces; to serve as such a member
   a. From the Latin *solidus*, a sum or piece of money that served as the soldier's pay
   b. From *scholder*, Old German, "to carry a musket"
   c. From the French *soldière*, meaning "a guard" or "protector"

225. **SOPHOMORE** A student in the second year of a course of study
   a. From Greek *sophosta*, "middle," as the usual courses in Greece were of three years' duration
   b. From Greek *sophos*, "wise," and *moros*, "foolish"; apparently, "a wise fool"
   c. From Sophomoros College in Greece, where students enrolled after one year at another school

226. **SORBONNE**   World-famous university in Paris, founded in 1253

   a. Via Old French, from Latin, *sorbonus,* meaning "to think philosophically"

   b. From the rue de Sorbonne, the street on which the students originally gathered to hear lectures

   c. From Robert de Sorbon, the founder of the school

227. **SOUVENIR**   A remembrance, either literally or figuratively; a memento

   a. Via the French, from the Latin, French meaning "to remember," Latin, "to come to mind"

   b. From the Old French *sous,* the plural of *sou,* "a small coin," meaning something purchased for very little as a trinket

   c. Origin unknown; probably French, but exact derivation uncertain

228. **SPOOF**   To hoax, to fool; a hoax

   a. From the German *spuffen,* "to wear a mask," thus indicating concealment of purpose

   b. From the name of a hoax game made up by Arthur Roberts (1852–1933)

   c. From the Old English *schpuff,* "ghost"

229. **SQUIRREL**   A rodent, arboreal and very active, with a long, bushy tail

   a. Via Latin from Greek, *skia-,* "shade," plus *oura,* "tail"

   b. From *Skirling,* the original name for the Norsemen who brought squirrels to England

   c. From *Skwerl,* late German, meaning "leaping animal"

230. **STALACTITE (1)/STALAGMITE (2)**   (1) A pendant, like an icicle, caused by evaporation of water percolating through limestone; (2) an upward-growing conical formation caused by the drip from a stalactite or from the roof

   a. From the Greek *stalagmos* and *stalactos,* meaning "a cave"

   b. From the Latin *stalactus,* with the middle syllable slightly changed, meaning "a cage" or "prison" (bars)

   c. From the Greek *stallassein,* "to drip"

231. **STRUDEL** A series of very thin layers of pastry, made into one sheet, which is used to enclose a filling, often of cheese or fruit, occasionally meat

   a. From the German *strudeln,* "to fill up with food"

   b. From Old Norse to German, from *skurdeln,* "to provide festive food," as strudel was served only at celebrations

   c. From the German *Struden,* meaning "eddy" or "whirlpool"

232. **STUPENDOUS** Astonishingly large, astonishing, astounding

   a. From the present participle of the Latin verb *stupere,* "to be stunned"

   b. A slang word of the fifteenth century (like "humongous" today, slang meaning "absolutely enormous"), which has become part of the language

   c. From the same root as stupid, because anything so large was considered to make one lose one's wits

233. **SUPERCILIOUS** Disdainful, superior, overbearing in manner

   a. From the Latin *super,* "above," and *cilium,* "eyelid"

   b. Despite the similarity to Latin, from the French *supricile,* meaning "a lord of the manor"

   c. Not specifically determined, apparently English slang in the time of Dr. Johnson, who lists it as current "cant" in his dictionary

234. **SUTTEE** The custom formerly observed in India of a wife's immolating herself on her husband's funeral pyre

   a. From a British misunderstanding of the Hindi word for death, *suetar*

   b. From the Sanskrit *suti,* "a true wife"

   c. A name attached to the custom by imaginative writers of Kipling's time because it "sounded" right

235. **SWITCH** A flexible rod; a form of changeover in railroading; the game of bridge; and further senses

   a. First recorded in Shakespeare as *switz,* but not in general use, apparently, before his time

   b. From the Old German *Schvitz,* "sweat," as produced by a beating with a switch

   c. From the Old English *schwitz,* meaning "a beating," usually punishment for a servant

236. **TABBY**   A cat with specific markings like damask silk; the fabric itself; a gossipy woman
  a.   From *tabard,* Middle English for "blouse," usually made of this sort of silk, hence transferred to a group of women gathered in their finery to gossip
  b.   From Tabis, the Egyptian cat goddess, who is portrayed in tomb paintings as having brindled markings
  c.   From the French *tabis* for this sort of silk fabric, apparently from Al-Attabiya, the section of Baghdad where the silk was made

237. **TABOO (or TABU)**   A system of prohibition regarding things that are holy or unclean; now extended to actions
  a.   From the Hebrew *tabo,* meaning "forbidden"
  b.   From the Latin *tabus,* a sacred shrine that ordinary people could not approach unless accompanied by a priest
  c.   From the Polynesian *taboo,* meaning "sacred" or "unclean," depending on the context

238. **TELLER**   In a bank, one whose duty it is to receive and count money
  a.   From the word *Thaler,* an old German coin
  b.   From *tellus, tellorum,* Latin, meaning "the collection of money in a bank"
  c.   From the German *zahlen,* "to number," through Old English *tellan*

239. **THEOBROMA**   The genus to which the chocolate or cacao (cocoa) tree belongs
  a.   From the area of South America where the plant was first discovered
  b.   From the two first names of the men who brought chocolate back to Europe, Theodore and Bromar
  c.   From the Greek *theo,* "god," and *broma,* "food"

240. **TIP**   A gratuity offered for service; a piece of information allegedly secret but passed on as a favor or warning
  a.   From the box kept outside old English taverns marked *To Insure Promptness,* where people dropped small change for the waiters or waitresses

    b.   Most dictionaries that give derivations list it as thieves' cant, to be understood as giving something special

    c.   Origin unknown

241. **TOWN** A village, an urban community, a municipal district

    a.   A corruption of "tower," as the cities were formerly guarded by walls and watchtowers

    b.   From the Latin *tonus,* "stones," representing the city walls

    c.   From the German, originally *Zaun,* "hedge," through Old English *tŭn,* "an enclosure"

242. **TOXIC** Poisonous or due to poison

    a.   From the Greek *toχon,* "a bow," and the compound *toχi-kon,* "an arrow poison"

    b.   From *toχos,* a poisonous plant growing in Asia Minor and recognized as fatal to humans by early peoples in that area

    c.   From Toxos, child of Thanos, Death, in Greek mythology

243. **TROY** A system of measurement—weights used for precious metal and gems; 5,760 grains divided into 12 ounces

    a.   From Troy in Asia Minor, where these weights were first used

    b.   From *troye,* the Old French term for certain precious stones

    c.   From Troyes, in France, where this system was apparently first developed

244. **TURQUOISE** A mineral, ranging from sky blue to green, opaque; the color, normally blue, of such a stone

    a.   From the American Indian word *turkos,* meaning "sky blue"

    b.   From Turkey, where such stones were originally found and imported to Europe

    c.   From the color, and the stone was named after a dye of that shade

245. **URANUS** A planet, discovered by Sir William Herschel in 1781; the father of Kronos and the Titans in Greek mythology

    a.   Named after the radioactive metal uranium, which had been discovered just before the planet was found

    b.   From the Greek *ouranos,* "heaven"

    c.   From an early Greek word adapted from Phoenician, meaning "shining"

246. URBANE Refined, civilized, well-mannered

   a. From Urbanus, a character in one of Shakespeare's plays, noted for his good manners

   b. From *urbis*, Latin, "a city," indicating that city dwellers were more refined than country folk

   c. From Old German *Oerbahn*, "well traveled," indicating a degree of polish and knowledge

247. UTILITARIAN Based on usefulness alone without regard to beauty, aesthetics, or similar considerations

   a. First coined by Jeremy Bentham, the British economist, as a back-formation from utility

   b. The standard adjectival form of utility, in use as long as utility has existed

   c. Developed by writers of the nineteenth century to describe a particular philosophy

248. VACCINE A preparation used to cause immunity to an illness or disease

   a. From vaccination, a word invented by Jenner for his injections against smallpox, from *vaccus*, "empty" (of disease)

   b. A made-up word with no derivation discernible

   c. From *vacca*, Latin for "cow," because the smallpox vaccine was developed originally from individuals who had contracted cowpox, a mild form of the same infection

249. VAIN Self-centered, conceited, with an overvalued self-image

   a. From the same root as *vein*, meaning "full of blood, puffed up"

   b. Definition unknown, first used by Chaucer in one of his early works, perhaps from *veir*, French for "fur"—as a nobleman dressed in fur

   c. From the Latin *vanus*, meaning "empty"

250. VAUDEVILLE Now a variety entertainment of songs and dances; a play with such songs and dances interspersed

   a. From the Vaudeville Theatre in London, where such musical variety shows first appeared in 1790 or thereabouts

   b. A coined word, made up to sound like the music and dance

c. From Vau de Vire, later Val de Vire, in France, where such musical entertainments and songs were apparently performed in the fifteenth century

251. **VEGETABLE** Generally, a plant, or part of one, used for food; normally grown in a fixed position, as distinguished from an animal

a. From the Latin for earth or ground developed the verb *vegetare,* meaning "to be rooted in the earth"

b. A misreading of an early Latin phrase by an English translator, but the original phrase describing such food is not known

c. From the Latin *vegetus, vegetabilit, vegetare,* "lively, animated, animating"

252. **VERMICELLI** A very thin form of pasta

a. From Vermicula, an old, formerly Roman city where this form of pasta was the specialty

b. From *vermis,* Latin for "worm"

c. From the Latin word meaning "little dish," the *-elli* being a diminutive

253. **VERNACULAR** The language of a particular group; the native language, slang, or idiom of a particular group

a. From Latin *verniculus,* "a home-born slave"

b. From the Frenchman I. Vernacula, who first translated a biblical section into the local language

c. From Vernacula, the city where literature was first printed in anything but Latin

254. **VICAR** Customarily, a clergyman of a particular status, especially in Great Britain

a. From *vicare,* Latin, meaning "to lead a flock"

b. From the Bible, as a title given to certain church officials

c. From the Latin *vicarius,* "a substitute" (same root as vicarious), as the clergyman is delegating for a higher official

255. **VOLT** Unit of electromotive force

a. From the Latin *volta,* "spark" or "electric spark" (sparks were known, though electricity was not understood)

b. Name invented by Benjamin Franklin following his kite experiments—based on "bolt" for lightning

    c.   From Alessandro Volta, 1745–1827, an Italian scientist

256. **WASSAIL**   A liquor with which healths were drunk; the festivities connected with such drinking

    a.   An abbreviation of "We all hail thee"

    b.   From the wassail bowl in which the drinks were kept, made in Wassal, western Scandinavia, originally

    c.   From Old Norse *ves heill,* "be in (good) health"

257. **WISTARIA**   A garden shrub, a climber of considerable beauty and magnificence, named by Thomas Nuttall, English naturalist

    a.   From the Wistar Gardens in Suffolk, where he naturalized the formerly wild American plant

    b.   From the earl of Wistar, in France, who brought the shrub home with him from a voyage

    c.   From Caspar Wistar (1761–1818), an American physician

258. **WORRY**   To trouble oneself, to be concerned to a great degree; as an active verb, to tear apart

    a.   From Old English *wrygan,* "to harm," same root as German *wurgan,* "to strangle"

    b.   From *wirer,* "to chew," Old Norse

    c.   Origin obscure, first appeared in the *Anglo-Saxon Chronicle*

259. **WRENCH**   An instrument for turning nuts, and so on; a twisting motion

    a.   From Old English *wrencan,* "to deceive"

    b.   From the original name of the nuts that needed a wrench to turn them, *wrenkum,* or "fastening nut" in Old Norse

    c.   From *wrangan,* "wagon" in Old English, as wrenches were first used to fix the wheels on carts or wagons

260. **XYLOPHONE**   A type of musical instrument consisting of a series of wooden bars, usually joined together by varying lengths of metal, which alter the tone produced when each bar is struck

    a.   From Xylophia, the daughter of the Muse of music, who, it is claimed, invented this instrument

    b.   From the Greek words *xylo* and *phone,* meaning "talking" or "speaking wood"

    c.   From John Richard Williams, English musician (1685–1735), who invented this type of instrument for the English stage and also invented the name

261. **YACHT**   Now, usually, an elegant pleasure boat (with the connotation of large expense), either sail or motor
   a. From the Old English *kyacht,* the name given to the royal barge in which the ruling family made voyages on the Thames
   b. From the French *yater,* "to sail," as certain types of sailboats were reserved for royalty or nobility
   c. Originally from the German *jagen,* "to hunt," through Dutch *jagt* and then *jacht*

262. **YTTRIUM**   A metallic element, atomic number 39, normally categorized as one of the rare earths
   a. From the name of the Norse god Yterry, who was supposed to live in the earth
   b. From Ignatz Yterr, 1789–1830, who discovered this particular rare earth on his father's farm and won scientific fame thereby
   c. From Ytterby, the quarry in Sweden where the element was first isolated

263. **ZEAL**   Enthusiasm, intensely expressed; strong feelings of support for a cause
   a. A back-formation from Zealot, a leader of a strongly defended cause in classical Greek times in Sparta: Zealots were the crack troops who defended the city
   b. A misreading in Middle English literature of the word *weal,* meaning "for the common good"
   c. From the Old French *zele,* Latin *zelus,* and Greek *zelos,* "to boil"

264. **ZINNIA**   A composite plant, multicolored, originally found in America
   a. From J. B. Zinn, botanist (1727–1759)
   b. From Zenobia, the Greek goddess, who was usually portrayed wearing the European version of this plant in her hair
   c. From Zenn, in Denmark, where the wildflower, as it was originally, was first naturalized and distributed, hence named after its place of cultivation

ANSWERS: CHAPTER 1

1. **ACADEMY**   c.   The grove, or garden, or location where Plato rented space for his academy was called Akademos, or Academos. Most dictionaries and references agree that it was the name of the man who owned the property. Nobody gives him a first name, or a last name, if Akademos was his first. All we are certain of is that it was his property, and that his name was given to Plato's school. Thus the landlord became almost more famous than the tenant, as there are certainly more uses of academy, academic, and the like than there are of Plato or platonic.

2. **ADMIRAL**   c.   The word was originally Arabic. It became confused, according to several dictionaries, somewhere along the way with the Latin word *admirare*, meaning "to admire," but it earlier was pure Arabic.

3. **AGNOSTIC**   c.   This one surprised the author. It does seem as if the word should have been in common usage for a long time, but the evidence shows that T. H. Huxley coined it when he could not find a specific English word to cover the attitude and philosophy he was contemplating. There is no earlier use than in his writings of 1869.

4. **ALGEBRA**   c.   This word too comes from the Arabic. The Arab notational system lent itself to such computations far more than did the Roman or Greek, and our entire mathematical system is based on arabic numerals.

5. **ALIBI**   a.   This word is a direct translation from the Latin, meaning "I was elsewhere." This was the original meaning of such a plea in court—that the defendant could prove he was not at the scene of the crime, hence could not have committed it. It has grown over the years to mean any excuse for anything, as in the old fictional character, "Alibi Ike," who always had an excuse for not doing something. This broader sense is a bit of a stretch for the actual meaning, but colloquial usage sanctions it.

6. **AMETHYST**   b.   The exact translation is a prevention against drunkenness. It is remarkable that despite the obvious failure

of the amethyst to do its assigned job, belief in this tradition persisted well into the Middle Ages.

7. AMOK b. It is a Malaysian term and seems to be a well-recognized syndrome there. Men apparently lose all restraint and commit multiple murders in a frenzied rage.

8. ANTIMACASSAR c. Macassar oil was very much beloved of the Victorians. It was wonderful hair grease, but it left an oily residue on everything it touched. So the careful housewife of that era knitted, crocheted, tatted, or made from fabric a nice, usually lacy, covering for the upper part of chairs. Eventually, as you will see if you look at pictures of Victorian homes, this craze spread to chair arms and sofa arms as well. Many of us probably have stored away, somewhere, our grandmothers' or great-grandmothers' antimacassars. They are often sold at rummage sales as dresser cloths or square runners, but they are probably antimacassars.

9. APERIENT c. This word is sometimes used in the sense of aperitif, but the actual meaning is that of laxative. The Romans didn't mince words and called things by their proper names. The dictionary we used gives aperitif as an alternate sense, but it would seem to be essential to discover whether you were being offered a genuine aperitif or a genuine aperient before you drank whatever it was.

10. ARCTIC c. It is the Greek for "bear." The search for this derivation led the author down several interesting byways, none of which reached any satisfactory ending. Was it called The Bear because the constellation Great Bear pointed to the north? Were the Greeks familiar with travelers' tales that told of bears in the far north? Was the climate sufficiently different that peoples who traded with the Greeks had seen polar bears, or even black bears or brown bears native to the far north? Probably those questions can never be answered.

11. ASSASSIN c. There was a particular sect that took hashish to commit ritual murders. "Thug" has the same derivation in a sect—the Thuggees—committed to ritual murders, with the name being transferred to any evil person. The Thuggees were wiped out in the early nineteenth century in India.

12. **ATLAS** b.　Atlas's picture appeared on the cover of the first collection of maps that was sold widely, and the book became known as an "Atlas." The name has just passed into popular usage from there.

13. **AURORA** a.　Aurora was one of the innumerable Roman deities. She had the dawn as her particular concern and was supposed to be a personification of the pink and glowing appearance of the sky at that time. The Romans had a god or goddess for everything, even for the sewers, a useful individual to pray to in order to help keep a city healthy, but a bit unusual.

14. **AZALEA** c.　The word means "dry soil." Apparently the Greeks believed that the flower or shrub grew best in dry or sandy soil.

15. **BADMINTON** c.　The game seems to have been developed there to amuse the duke and his friends. As it spread in popularity, of course, it became known by the name of the estate where it had been invented.

16. **BAGATELLE** c.　The word is Old French or Italian, meaning "a trick" or "a trifle." There *is* a Bagatelle Palace in the Bois de Boulogne in Paris, so called because it is tiny and because it was put up on a bet in a very short period of time.

17. **BALDACHIN** c.　The famous baldachin or baldaquin in St. Peter's is not made of cloth, but the earliest ones were. They were made of particularly sumptuous material, which came from the Near East—Baghdad—called in Italian Baldacco. The name of the place of origin was transferred to the cloth, and then to the object.

18. **BALLOT** c.　It's a "small ball." For many years, balloting was done by dropping a small ball into a box—black for no, white for yes. That's where the expression "blackball" came from. If a club member wished to stop someone from joining, all he had to do was drop in a black ball, and the disliked person could not be made a member. Balloting is merely a variant of this procedure.

19. **BARBARIAN** a.　If you weren't a Greek or a Roman, your speech was incomprehensible, hence "stammering." Different languages use similar expressions. After all, in English we say,

when we don't understand the explanation or the words, "It's Greek to me!"

20. BASCULE b. From the French word for seesaw, which is exactly what a bascule bridge does when it is in operation.

21. BEDLAM b. Bethlehem became Bedlam quite early. If Magdalen College can be pronounced "Maudlin," and Cirencester "Sister" or "Sisiter," this contraction is not very surprising.

22. BIBLE a. All books were originally written on papyrus. When the Book was written, the name was applied to it by a process of synecdoche.

23. BLAZER a. The original blazers were always a brilliant red.

24. BOWDLERIZE a. The ineffable Dr. Bowdler decided that Shakespeare was much too vulgar and published an edited and cleaned-up version in ten volumes at the beginning of the nineteenth century.

25. BOYCOTT b. Captain Boycott is forgotten as a person but the word lives on. He was so thoroughly ostracized from all human connection that he finally gave up and moved away.

26. BUNKUM b. According to several dictionaries, this is the correct answer. It is one of those words, however, for which there seem to be several stories extant. The author took the version agreed on by two major dictionaries.

27. BURNOUT a, b, and c. We really don't know when the term for emotional fatigue and inability to function came into use, but it seems to have appeared with the current rocket era.

28. CABOCHON c. The root word is Latin *caput*, "head." There is a similar word in heraldry, caboshed, meaning a face with no neck showing. In this case, obviously, the gem was considered to be all head, or top.

29. CALCULATE c. It's Latin—the original meaning, derived from "little stone," was to do mathematical computations by means of little stones. If you could not read or write numbers, it was far simpler to count your sheep by putting a stone in one spot for each sheep you drove into the pen.

30. CAMELLIA c. The Moravian Jesuit priest was Kamel. His name, Latinized, is Camellus. He seems to have been the in-

dividual who introduced this particular Far Eastern plant to the Western world and, in return, had it named for him.

31. CATECHISM   c.   The word originally did not have any religious connotation, simply meaning the incessant repetition of questions and answers.

32. CHAUVINISM   a.   Nicolas Chauvin it was. He was both admired and laughed at for intense and unwavering devotion to France and to his leader, Napoleon. The word has also come to have connotations of xenophobia, or dislike of foreigners, and has lost most of the admiration once attached to it.

33. CHESS   c.   Originally it comes from the Persian. It has come down through many European languages in varied forms. In French, as has happened with many words starting in *s*, an *e* appeared in front of the word, producing *echec;* in German it became *Schach* and in Italian, *schacci.* But the game seems to have started in Persia, as it was then, as a war game with kings as the chief protagonists.

34. CHICANERY   b.   This word comes from the Persian for "crooked mallet." It has a long history, starting with a mallet game in which, obviously, using a crooked mallet would be cheating. From there, it descended through several European languages, losing the connotation of a game along the way, but maintaining the connotation of trickery.

35. CLINK   c.   The most authoritative sources indicate that the slang usage of the word comes from the Clink Prison, on Clink Street. A good deal of British slang, especially London slang, made its way into American usage, and this word seems to be one example. Clink Street and the site of the prison both still exist.

36. CLOCK   c.   It is derived from the Latin word for bell. Of course, the earliest clocks had no hands. The original city clocks were bells that tolled the hours, which were the only means available. The Greek water clocks, the sand timers, and similar devices had no hands.

37. COACH   c.   Kocs in Hungary is what the origin seems to be. The carriages were apparently first made there.

38. COBALT   b.   It is indeed *Kobold,* or wicked imp or sprite, from the German. It is unclear from the dictionaries and reference books whether the miners actually ran into a form of radioactive cobalt and recognized its danger or whether it was just a particularly difficult type of mine with collapsing walls and ceilings, but it was believed that the mines were inhabited by these evil spirits.

39. COFFEE   a.   From the Arabic, through Turkey: it isn't quite clear when or how the meaning changed, but the word "coffee" has been used to describe the drink and the bean we now know for many hundreds of years.

40. COPPER   c.   The metal was originally found in Cyprus.

41. CURFEW   b.   All fires had to be covered at night, for safety's sake, and a watchman gave warning of the proper time to do so.

42. *d*   c.   After all, the Romans occupied England for more than four centuries, and some of their customs lasted longer. The abbreviations *d* for *denarius* and £ for *libra,* pound, lasted another thirteen hundred years or so.

43. DAGUERREOTYPE   b.   Louis Daguerre (1789–1851) helped develop this type of photography on copper plates. His partner was Mr. Niepce (niepceotype?), who passed from the scene much earlier.

44. DAHLIA   b.   The plant was named by Linnaeus, the Swedish taxonomist, after a friend and pupil, Anders Dahl.

45. DAMASK   c.   The name comes from Damascus, where the material was originally made; also, of course, Damascus steel.

46. DELTA   c.   The mouth of the Nile was shaped like the Greek capital letter delta, so the term was applied first to that particular river mouth, and afterward to all.

47. DISASTER   c.   From the French, via Latin and Greek, the meaning is "from an evil star." We still use the expression in a slightly different form, when we say "star-crossed" to mean someone who is unlucky.

48. DOILY   b.   It comes from an English haberdasher, according to three authoritative sources, but more than that is not given.

49. DOLLAR   b.   The word's origin is the German *Thaler,* short for *Joachimsthaler,* as it was first coined in Bohemia at a place called Joachimsthal. From there it became *Thaler* and passed into a good many languages as "dollar."

50. DYNAMITE   c.   The origin is the Greek word meaning "power." From the same root come dynamo, dynamic, and several others, all of which basically convey the idea of power.

51. EARL   c.   "Earl" is the same as the Old English *eorl,* "warrior," coming down from Old Norse, *jarl,* "a hero," usually in battle.

52. ELEPHANT   c.   The word *olfand* in Old English means "a camel." Apparently, to the Old English, any strange beast was the same!

53. ENEMY   a.   "Enemy" comes from the Latin *in* (not) and *amicus* (a friend)—the same source as the word "amiable."

54. ENGINEER   c.   The root is Latin *ingenium,* "skill."

55. ENIGMA   b.   The word combines the Greek terms meaning "to speak darkly" and "a fable."

56. EPIDEMIC   b.   The origin is Greek: *epi,* "among," and *demos,* "the people."

57. FACET   c.   The source is the French "little face," or *facette.*

58. FAHRENHEIT   b.   Gabriel Fahrenheit invented this scale, which remained in general use until the Centigrade-Celsius unit came into the picture.

59. FAUNA   c.   In particular, the Latin deities Fauna and Faunus represented shepherds (and shepherdesses, too).

60. FOMALHAUT   b.   Arabic—the whale's mouth—is the source of this name, because it is in the constellation called the Southern Fish.

61. FORENSIC   a.   From Latin, *forensis, forum,* "the marketplace," thus "courts"; trials were held there by the Romans so that everyone could see justice done.

62. FORUM   b.   It is a Latin loanword originally meaning "out-of-doors," where it was more feasible to meet in Rome than in England or the northern United States, for example.

63. FRANC   c.   The legend *francorum rex*—or king of the

French—appeared on the first coins. As usual, everyone found a convenient abbreviation for an everyday object in common use.

64. GALAXY b. The root is the Greek word for milk and thus, by extension, the Milky Way.

65. GAMBIT c. "Gambit" has its origins indeed in the Italian, in the sense of "tripping up" or putting a leg in front of someone to make him fall. There was originally an element of trickery in the use of the word, which shows in its root.

66. GARDENIA b. Of course, the dates of his birth and death show that Dr. Garden wasn't an American when he was born; but he did live in the United States when it was founded, and he did name the plant.

67. GAS a. This one is rather surprising, as it is generally not considered to be a coined word. Von Helmont invented it, or devised it, or coined it, and drew his inspiration from the Greek *chaos*, with the same basic meaning it has today.

68. GERANIUM b. The source is Greek and Latin, *geranion/geranus*, "a crane."

69. GOURMET b. It comes from the French, originally meaning a winemaker's assistant. It is not listed in most dictionaries as an adjective, but as a noun. Its use to describe various foods or styles of cooking or eating is of fairly recent origin.

70. GRAVITY c. It is directly descended from the Latin, meaning "heavy."

71. GUBERNATORIAL c. This word is yet another derivation from the Latin, "one who steers." The Romans seem to have had some firm ideas about the roles their officials were supposed to play.

72. GUILLOTINE c. The machine we now know as a guillotine was apparently invented in Italy. No reference book gives Dr. Guillotin credit for inventing it. He popularized its use for humane purposes, as he was apparently sickened by some of the methods of execution used at that time. When it became so widely used during the French Revolution and his name was adopted to describe it, he was equally horrified. He lived until 1814—was not guillotined by the machine he championed—

and hated the use of the name. According to a fairly widely documented story, his family petitioned the French government to change the name of the machine after his death. This the government would not do, so the family did the next best thing: they changed *their* name. The name they adopted is, as might be expected, unknown.

73. GUNITE   a.   The name was originally trademarked, but the company seems to have lost this protection, and it is now listed as "formerly trademarked."

74. HACIENDA   c.   The original owners of haciendas had a realistic view of the world, apparently. Today the word is used to mean a Spanish-style house out in the country, but the original meaning carried the definite implication of work.

75. HALCYON   a.   The original story was that the bird possessed magical powers to calm the sea during its nesting period. The word has altered slightly to mean any happy, peaceful time.

76. HANSOM   b.   From the inventor, Joseph A. Hansom. (There is a whole group of words that originated in the public transportation of that period—cab for cabriolet; bus for omnibus [to carry all]; car for motorcar.)

77. HAZARD   a.   Apparently this word reached Europe via the Crusades.

78. HEAVISIDE LAYER   b.   This is an eponymous name from its discoverer, Oliver Heaviside (1850–1925). It is merely fortuitous that the gentleman's name sounds as if it is connected to a heavy layer of atmosphere.

79. KIOSK   c.   This one got to us from the Near East, where garden pavilions were both useful and usable.

80. KOWTOW   a.   The Chinese used the word, in the form given, to mean a show of respect.

81. LADY   c.   Despite the current connotation of gentility attached to the word, it originally meant the dough kneader in the household, or the female in charge of the house, of course. Lord originally meant the bread guardian.

82. LANTHANUM   b.   As it was not discovered until fairly late, and in rather rare minerals, the classically trained scientists of that date used the Greek root to name it.

83. LARVA   c.   It comes from the Greek word for mask, as the immature form masked the later development.

84. LAUDANUM   a.   It is from the Latin. The discovery of pain-killing drugs was a major advance. See the derivation of such phrases as "bite the bullet" for an example of what happened before pain-killers.

85. LAVALIERE   c.   This unfortunate lady (also sometimes spelled Lavalliere) was the rather unhappy mistress of Louis XIV. When she fell out of favor, she retired to a convent and spent the rest of her life there. She apparently had not sought the king's favor, nor did she much wish it. She did, however, leave her name on the type of necklace she often wore.

86. LEFT   c.   It comes from the word meaning "paralysis." Left-handed individuals have suffered some discrimination in most languages; for example, *sinistra*, from which we get "sinister," is the Latin for "left."

87. LEISURE   a.   Latin is responsible once more. Obviously, "it is permitted" not to work.

88. LIMOUSINE   c.   There's a small museum in the town of Limousin showing the derivation of coach body types.

89. LINOLEUM   a.   Mr. Walton patented linoleum in 1860 and 1863. He derived the name from (b), the Latin for *linum*, "flax" and *oleum*, "oil."

90. LOFT   c.   The source is *luft*, "the air."

91. LONGAN   b.   This delicious and exotic fruit was named by the Chinese. Available mostly canned in the United States in oriental food stores, it can be found fresh in ethnic areas.

92. LOOT   c.   Originally from Hindi, its route into English is not clearly traced.

93. LUDO   c.   It comes directly from Latin with no intermediaries. The game must have been named by a Latinist.

94. LUTE   a.   The name originated in an Arabic-speaking country.

95. LUTETIA   c.   Several reference works say "mud," but some others say "city surrounded by water," which may sound somewhat more romantic.

96. LYNCH   c.   An eponymous word.

97. **MACABRE** b. Three dictionaries agree that the source is Hebrew.

98. **MACADAM** b. John Loudon McAdam invented it. He was *not* the same as Macadam, who found the macadamia nut, which is why his middle name is given.

99. **MACH** c. No possible disagreement: all dictionaries and encyclopedias, not to mention scientific texts, give Ernst Mach credit for this one.

100. **MAGENTA** b. According to the dictionaries, the dye was discovered about the time of the Battle of Magenta, so it was called magenta. No explanation states why a color should be named after a battle.

101. **MAGNET** a. This seems to have been a magnetic stone, the properties of which were discovered by the Romans.

102. **MAGNOLIA** c. Despite the plausible-sounding alternatives, it was Pierre Magnol.

103. **MAILLOT** c. It's French, it did mean "swaddling clothes," as the bathing suit fitted so tightly. Lately, advertising has unfortunately used the nonword *mio*, based on the pronunciation *my-OH*. Of course *mio*, as used, would be pronounced *MEE-oh*, as in "O sole mio."

104. **MALAPROPISM** c. Sheridan undoubtedly took the name of his character Mrs. Malaprop from the French expression.

105. **MAMMON** b. The word is sometimes capitalized, both in daily use and in the Bible, as if it were the name of a pagan god or spirit, but it is not.

106. **MANGY** b. The root sense is "chewed up," as the Latin originally meant, because of the appearance, especially of a dog losing hair in patches.

107. **MANSION** c. This term has had numerous meanings through the years, but there does not seem to be much disagreement that it comes originally from the Latin *manere*.

108. **MAP** b. Very specifically it is from the Latin meaning "napkin" or "painted cloth," with some evidence that it was originally Punic. This derivation, of course, leads one to speculate whether the Romans doodled on tablecloths and napkins.

109. **MAQUIS** a. The derivation is fairly clear. The shrub is ex-

tremely dense and forms an almost impenetrable web or mesh of branches.

110. MARASCHINO   c.   This one too comes almost directly from the Latin. Originally, of course, the liqueur was Maraschino and the cherries were macerated in it, but eventually the term came to be applied to the artificially dyed, no liqueur, cherries used for cocktails and other concoctions.

111. MARKET   b.   It is derived from merchandise and trading. There were laws about taxes and about trading, but they had nothing to do with the boundaries of a selling area.

112. MARMALADE   b.   One source became very scornful about the derivation quoted in (a), which is folklore, because of the fact that a Scottish queen spoke French, or that French was spoken about her. But because Mary, Queen of Scots, was married in her teens to the heir to the French throne and spoke perfect French, it is not as silly as it sounds at first.

113. MAROON   a.   The nut gave the color its name.

114. MARSHAL   c.   This word has changed meaning slightly, but not enough to put it in the chapter about words that have nearly reversed their meanings.

115. MARTINET   b.   From General Martinet: it is just a coincidence that the Roman god of war was named Mars.

116. MASOCHISM   b.   Sacher-Masoch's name is often combined with that of the marquis de Sade to form the term "sado-masochism," though they lived at different times.

117. MATADOR   a.   Originally it was a sacrificial kill, honoring someone or something. It is the word "toreador," often used in translations of *Carmen,* that is really not accurate.

118. MATRICULATE   b.   *Matricula* meant "a register."

119. MATTRESS   a.   The source is Arabic *matrah,* meaning "a place where things are thrown."

120. MAUSOLEUM   c.   The term passed into general use because it was the most magnificent tomb known at that date.

121. MAYDAY   c.   The term comes from the French for "help me," though why it was chosen has not been satisfactorily explained.

122. MEANDER   a.   The river wound around and had such twists

and turns that the word came to signify anything in the way of a walk or a path with these characteristics.

123. MEERSCHAUM   b.   The early Germans indeed thought this clay was solidified sea-foam. This notion has been verified from several sources, as it seemed a little difficult to accept at first.

124. MELANCHOLY   b.   The Greeks believed in the four humors, which composed human temperaments, and this was one of them. Somebody full of black bile would not be very happy.

125. MENACE   b.   The source is the Latin *minaciae*, "threats," as a loose roof coping or building corner would be, in a very real sense.

126. MENTOR   b.   The wise and learned counselor of Telemachus was named Mentor.

127. MESMERIZE   a.   Mesmer believed that he could cure many illnesses by this method. His name passed into the literature in a figurative as well as a literal way.

128. METICULOUS   b.   It comes from the Latin for "frightened." Someone who is excessively careful is afraid of making a mistake.

129. MIGRAINE   c.   The Greeks had a word for it.

130. MILE   a.   The Romans were road builders par excellence and needed to know such things as standardized measurements.

131. MILLINER   c.   Very often goods were named for their place of origin.

132. MINIATURE   a.   The pseudo-resemblance to *mini* has made the word take on a meaning of its own, but the original derivation was from the red lead paint used for illuminating manuscripts.

133. MISERICORD   b.   The older and more infirm members of the congregation could lean against these semiseats. (In some cathedrals, there are scatalogical carvings under the misericords in the darkest corners. With no light except candles in a dark cathedral, the evil-minded workmen could enjoy their little joke in the security of knowing that nobody would ever see the details—vide Lincoln Cathedral in England, which has a large assortment.)

134. MNEMONIC   c.   The goddess was responsible.

135. **MOB** a. The Latin term implied a volatile crowd.

136. **MOHOLE** c. This is "hole," obviously, and "Mo" to commemorate Andrija Mohorovičić, who was Croatian and presented his theory about layers in the Earth's crust in 1909.

137. **MONEY** c. Juno had a good many surnames, according to what attribute was being emphasized at the moment, and Moneta was one of them, assigned to her temple where money was coined.

138. **MORPHINE** c. Again, it was a Greek god, Morpheus. Some classically inclined people say "in the arms of Morpheus" when they mean "asleep."

139. **MORTGAGE** c. The pledge is dead once you have paid off the mortgage, or the loan.

140. **MUSCLE** a. Thought to bear a resemblance to a small mouse, it must be assumed; but that is a rather large assumption for a rather small mouse.

141. **MUSTARD** b. The Romans made mustard with much the same ingredients as we do today.

142. **NADIR** c. The root is the opposite of the top, which is the zenith.

143. **NARCISSUS** c. The young Narcissus is supposed to have pined away, looking at himself. One of the deities took pity on him and changed him into a flower.

144. **NASTURTIUM** c. The pungent odor is very much disliked by many people.

145. **NAUSEA** c. Seasickness. The Greeks often wrote of the discomforts of sea travel, as the Mediterranean can be very rough.

146. **NEIGHBOR** b. Originally it meant "a nearby farm," now extrapolated.

147. **NEON** b. Ramsey called it after the Greek word for "new."

148. **NEWS** a. In the sense of "reports" or "tidings," the dictionaries give the Middle English derivation, as shown. Choice (b), while an amusing folktale, has no verifiable source. That doesn't mean people won't give it as the derivation, of course.

149. **NICKEL** c. The German miners were looking for copper, thought they took copper ore out, and found no copper. The

evil spirits did it. (Incidentally, it is *never* spelled "nickle," not even in pumpernickel.)

150. NICOTINE   a.   Jean Nicot (1530–1600) sent the leaves of the plant to Catherine de Medicis as a present, and she reciprocated by calling the product "nicotine."

151. NOON   a.   The day started at midnight, and nones were morning prayers.

152. OCEAN   a.   The Greeks had a word for everything, including this one.

153. ORIENT   c.   In this instance, the Latin derivative is the source. It is from the Latin verb *oriri,* referring to the direction in which the sun rose.

154. OUNCE   c.   It's those Romans again. We don't use troy weight much except for such items as gold.

155. OXYGEN   c.   Despite the logical-sounding explanation in (a), this one comes from the Greek. The Greeks did indeed believe that all acids included oxygen as a component.

156. PALACE   c.   The Palatine Hill was the home of palaces, and the adjectival form came to be used for such royal residences.

157. PAPER   a.   The original paper was papyrus, which the Egyptians had learned to make from the paper reed growing abundantly along the Nile.

158. PARAFFIN   b.   This is the correct explanation.

159. PARAPHERNALIA   c.   It has come a long way, but originally paraphernalia were the possessions a married woman could claim as her own. Everything else belonged to her husband.

160. PEDAGOGUE   c.   While "pediatrician" comes originally from the basic root word for children, a pedagogue was the very specific person who led a boy (girls were not included in the educational system in this manner) to his schooling.

161. PEN   a.   Of course, the original pens were sharpened quills. This usage lasted a mere two thousand years.

162. PERSON   b.   The actor's mask eventually came to mean the character behind the mask and, by extension, the person.

163. PLIMSOLL LINE   b.   Samuel Plimsoll has a very nice statue in the Embankment Gardens in London. His bright idea saved

thousands of lives, as it provided an easy way to determine the proper loading of a ship.

164. POINSETTIA   c.   Our minister to Mexico liked this lovely plant and brought it back to the United States. Incidentally, those lovely colored leaves are just that, leaves, not blossoms.

165. POLITE   c.   It comes from the Latin word meaning "to polish," so that the expression "polished manners" is as redundant as shrimp scampi.

166. POPLIN   c.   We aren't absolutely certain, but there is a fair amount of evidence to indicate that the fabric was woven in Avignon during the time that the popes resided there.

167. PORPOISE   b.   The resemblance may not be apparent to us, but the Romans thought they saw it and called the porpoise a hog-fish.

168. PRALINE   c.   This tasty confection, the mainstay of many candy shops in New Orleans, was invented at the French court. Apparently the development of a new delicacy for the pampered court palates was a highly significant event. There are many dishes named this way in the current language of cuisine.

169. PRECOCIOUS   c.   The source is the Latin for cooking or ripening; but of course, dementia praecox comes from the same root. It meant early madness, and was often applied to some forms of schizophrenia, which manifest themselves in late adolescence or early adulthood.

170. PREJUDICE   a.   The word is directly descended from French and Latin, meaning "wrong judgment."

171. PREVARICATE   a.   From the Latin meaning "walk crookedly"; in common usage, it has become a polite word for "lie."

172. PROFILE   a.   The original Latin meaning was of a thread, as the first profiles seem to have been just outlines or drawing lines.

173. PTOMAINE   b.   The root is the Greek word meaning "a corpse." We use the word quite loosely today for any kind of major stomach upset, but technically this is not correct.

174. PUCK (or POOK)   b.   The word seems to be of Scandinavian

and Celtic origin. Some books state that this is a friendly name for what was really quite an evil spirit who had to be placated.

175. PUNCH b. The British brought this drink home from the East, so the Hindi word for "five" is a very probable derivation, but it cannot be demonstrated. There is no evidence at all for either of the other two explanations. This author made them up after a glass of punch.

176. PUPIL (1) a. Again, it is the Latin for a boy or girl, with the word used in the diminutive.

177. PUPIL (2) b. The origin is the same, with a totally different meaning today.

178. PUPPET b. Again, it is the diminutive for girl, but with still another change in meaning.

179. PUPPY a. Once more, we have still another derivation of a word meaning "little girl" or "boy," here transferred to the animal kingdom. (These four totally different words, all with the same derivation, were included as an interesting curiosity and an indication of how the same root shows up in many different forms.)

180. PYREX (TM) c. This is a made-up name indicating that the glass was superior and fire resistant.

181. QUARANTINE c. The medieval world believed that if a disease did not show itself within forty days, the individual was safe. Ships coming from plague areas were therefore kept in the harbor, and nobody was allowed to land for that period of time.

182. QUICK a. This is the basis for the expression "the quick and the dead," meaning the living and the dead; also "quickening," meaning "coming to life."

183. RAW c. This one is from Old English. Many of our words relating to food in its uncooked state are Old English—the ones relating to cooked and served food are mostly from the French—a direct result of the differences between Saxon servants and Norman-French masters, following the takeover of William the Conquerer.

184. REEF c. The Norwegians, skilled boatmen, sailed from Nor-

way to many other countries, including England and France, in their small open boats. They knew the waters intimately.

185. REHEARSE   c.   This one comes from the Latin, and then the French, meaning to rerake, or reharrow; in short, going over work again and again.

186. RELENT   c.   The correct Latin source is "sticky" or "sluggish."

187. REMORSE   a.   The pangs of conscience were apparently known even back in Roman days, as they described remorse as being bitten again.

188. RHAPSODY   b.   The Greeks seem to have considered this type of music as a stitching together of songs, and that literal meaning has come down to us.

189. RIALTO   c.   It is a contraction of the Italian *rialzato*, "raised." The bridge is very much raised, not a flat span across. The term has passed into the language so thoroughly that many do not realize that the word was used for a place of commerce as far back as Shakespeare's day.

190. RIBBON   c.   Once in a while, a very common term shows up in the dictionary as "origin obscure or unknown." There are apparently no facts available to tell us the source of this word.

191. RITZY   c.   It was Mr. Ritz, who by a happy accident had a name that sounded like elegance and luxury.

192. ROBE   b.   The Old French it is, meaning "plunder" or "booty."

193. RODENT   b.   It comes from the Latin word meaning "to gnaw." That is the mammal's characteristic behavior in eating, because of the tooth formation.

194. ROOK   c.   Many chess terms like this one come from the Eastern countries, as the game apparently originated there.

195. ROSTER   b.   It is derived from the word for gridiron, because of the lines.

196. ROUÉ   c.   That is the explanation given in several dictionaries, with no further explanation. Perhaps Prince Philippe meant that they deserved to be broken on the wheel.

197. RUBRIC   a.   Here is another instance of the color used for

the original item being transferred as a name to the whole class of items (compare "miniature").

198. SABOTAGE b. The term was widely applied during World War II, and not just to people in *sabots*.

199. SALARY c. Many people could be self-sufficient, except for salt, in early Roman times. That had to be bought and paid for—so "salt money" was the term for wages.

200. SALMON b. Apparently the Romans had a species of salmon that they could see leaping upstream.

201. SARCASM c. The Greeks had a poetic way with words. Sarcasm does indeed tear at the flesh the way dogs do.

202. SATURN b. The Latin verb meaning "to sow" indicated the function of this god. The description of temperament came from alleged influences of the planet, not the other way around.

203. SAXIFRAGE a. That is what Pliny reported. No other medical studies have confirmed this claim, but the name has stuck.

204. SCANDAL b. Again, the literal meaning has come down to us figuratively. A scandal is indeed a stumbling block to advancement personally or professionally.

205. SCATTER a. The first appearance seems to be the *Anglo-Saxon Chronicle*. People seem to have made up words to fit situations.

206. SCHEDULE b. It doesn't seem much like papyrus, but there was a specific word for a strip of papyrus, as opposed to the whole sheet.

207. SCRUTINY a. Apparently, when you scrutinize an expense account closely, you are actually sifting through the rags, or the scrap.

208. SEA b. Although the Phoenicians sound plausible, the word is actually Norse in origin.

209. SEARCH b. In other words, the Romans considered a search to involve going around in a circle!

210. SECURE a. It means just not to worry, in other words.

211. SELTZER a. The water and the name are from Nieder Selters in Prussia.

212. SENATE b. It is the Latin for "old man"; from the same root come senile and senility.

213. SERENADE   a.   A bright, clear sky must have been the mental picture of a lover singing under his lady's window, which would be a rather disagreeable chore in the rain.

214. SHAKE   a.   This is Old English.

215. SHAMROCK   a.   This one was really too easy, but at least one of the alternates sounded plausible.

216. SHOP   b.   The root is Old English, as are many words with *sh*, in this case meaning "a treasury."

217. SHRAPNEL   a.   General Shrapnel deserves the credit, or discredit, for having invented this particular way of killing people.

218. SHUTTLE   b.   The shuttle "shoots" across the loom, and the word was derived from the old word meaning "dart" or "arrow," to mimic its motion.

219. SIESTA   c.   It comes from the Latin for sixth hour, probably the time that the Romans took naps.

220. SILHOUETTE   c.   Here we have yet another person who turned into a thing, though we really do not know quite why a French official of that period would have his name attached to this kind of portrait.

221. SIRLOIN   b.   Despite the long-time popularity of the folk legend about Queen Elizabeth knighting this cut of meat (even reprinted on some restaurant menus!), the name is a prosaic description of the exact location of the cut.

222. SLAVE   c.   Apparently this derivation came about because Slavs constituted the bulk of the slave labor at the time the word came into English.

223. SOAR   a.   This is another word from the Latin, meaning "to rise into the air."

224. SOLDIER   a.   The pay of a soldier was apparently a particular Roman coin, and the name was eventually transferred to the person receiving the money.

225. SOPHOMORE   b.   A "wise fool" it is, having learned more, apparently, than the first-year students but not as much as the student will know when he finishes.

226. SORBONNE   c.   Robert de Sorbon, the first teacher at this now world-famous university, gave his name to the school.

227. SOUVENIR   a.   The word is taken from the French and originally from the Latin, meaning "to remember."

228. SPOOF   b.   It is hard to imagine that this word is so new, but it did not exist prior to the invention of the game by Mr. Roberts.

229. SQUIRREL   a.   Despite the many plausible-sounding alternatives, several of which I like better than the actual derivation, the name means "shady tail."

230. STALACTITE/STALAGMITE   c.   The root word is the same for both. Stalactites are formed by drips from the ceiling that cling to a projection and do not drop farther, and stalagmites by drips from a stalactite or the ceiling (remember *c* for ceiling, *g* for ground).

231. STRUDEL   c.   For an unknown reason, it descends directly from the German meaning "eddy" or "whirlpool"—possibly whirlpool because of the multiple circles visible when it is cut.

232. STUPENDOUS   a.   It is derived from the Latin meaning "to be stunned." "Humongous" seems to have started spontaneously, but "stupendous" has a verifiable history.

233. SUPERCILIOUS   a.   Someone who is supercilious is raising an eyebrow at you, or looking at you with lifted and sneering brows.

234. SUTTEE   b.   It comes from the Sanskrit for "true wife."

235. SWITCH   a.   Shakespeare seems to have made up many words to fit his needs. Either he was a word coiner par excellence, or early transcribers made even more errors than those usually accepted.

236. TABBY   c.   The appearance of the silk was transferred to the mottled appearance of the cat. Of course, the use of the word to mean a gossip possibly arises from the fact that many women had pet cats and the cats sat around while the group of women gossiped.

237. TABOO   c.   The Polynesian tribes were overloaded with taboos relating to who could marry whom, who could speak with whom, the exact relationships of in-laws, and so forth. The word was so convenient and filled an unfilled niche in

English so thoroughly that it was immediately picked up as an English word.

238.   TELLER   c.   The word basically means "count." The ancient use of the word persists in such English usages as bank teller, telling beads, and others.

239.   THEOBROMA   c.   The Europeans who first tasted chocolate—as a drink, basically—were so struck by its delicious taste that the classically educated leaders of expeditions at that time named it the food of the gods.

240.   TIP   b.   This answer, thieves' cant, is apt to bring me all kinds of letters insisting that it really means "to insure promptness." That legend, along with "cop" meaning "constable on patrol" and similar folk etymologies, dies hard. The expression "tip" is recorded as slang among thieves and highwaymen over the past several hundred years, referring to giving someone a useful bit of advice. "Tip him off" still exists in this sense. The *Oxford English Dictionary* gives slang and cant as the probable origin, as do *Chambers Twentieth Century Dictionary* and many other standard reference works. All of them dismiss "to insure promptness" as folklore, as there is no evidence to support it. (To prevent any further correspondence, I will mention here that I have omitted "posh," which many people believe means "*P*ort *O*ut, *S*tarboard *H*ome," from the P. and O. Line's arrangements for important passengers. The P. and O.'s official disclaimer, printed in several books, has not sufficed to kill this one, so I'm leaving it out.)

241.   TOWN   c.   This one is German in origin, meaning "an enclosure." Obviously, the first settlements were enclosed for safety against animals as well as marauding humans. It is a little hard to realize, but until a few hundred years ago wild boars roamed the thick forests of Europe, and it was crucial to keep them out of the enclosed areas where children played and people worked.

242.   TOXIC   a.   From the Greek for "poisoned arrow": it is a common form of death in Greek and other mythology, and ob-

viously there would be a word to represent this fatal blow. It has since been transferred to anything that could be fatal.

243. TROY   c.   This type of measurement, originating in Troyes, is the key to the old riddle, "Which weighs more, a pound of gold or a pound of feathers?" Of course, the gold is weighed in the troy weight of only twelve ounces to the pound.

244. TURQUOISE   b.   It is surprising how many people believe that turquoise is an American Indian stone. It was first found in Turkey long before the Americas were found by Europeans and the Indian jewelry became famous.

245. URANUS   b.   Because of the position Uranus held in the Greek pantheon, his name meant "heaven." (Don't forget to accent that first syllable.)

246. URBANE   b.   The root is the word for city. The idea that city dwellers are more polished and more civilized shows up in many words. Those describing country people are usually somewhat derogatory and include the idea that country folk are rough, rude, and uncivilized. The Greeks and the Romans had a strong predilection for city life, interspersed with visits to the country, where they could rhapsodize about nature— but not the country people—and then return to the comforts of Athens or Rome.

247. UTILITARIAN   a.   Jeremy Bentham, the founder of Utilitarianism, coined the word. On his death, he gave a conspicuous example of nonutilitarian behavior by demanding in his will that his corpse sit at all board meetings. For a long period thereafter his corpse, fully dressed and with a top hat, sat in its usual place at meetings as a not-very-utilitarian director of the organization.

248. VACCINE   c.   It is taken from *vacca,* "cow." Jenner had noticed that the milkmaids who got cowpox never got smallpox and developed the idea of vaccination against smallpox from this observation. Now, of course, vaccines can be directed against many diseases.

249. VAIN   c.   The word comes from the Latin *vanus,* "empty."

250. VAUDEVILLE   c.   Although it sounds as if one of the other

definitions should be correct, there is good evidence that this form of entertainment originated in this locale and that the names of all the theaters came from there.

251. VEGETABLE a. Obviously, it springs from the original meaning of "to grow" (from seed, for example). A tiny, almost invisible seed can produce a large plant. The lack of sensory perceptions (as far as we know) and the immobility of plants has led to the popular or slang meaning of a dull or mentally destroyed person, who is sometimes described as merely a "vegetable."

252. VERMICELLI b. Latin had no hesitation about using extremely descriptive words for things, even food. It is entirely possible that some readers will have difficulty in eating vermicelli again, once they know it means "little worms." It is always possible to switch to *capellini d'angeli,* or angel's hair, a slightly thinner version.

253. VERNACULAR a. The root is the Latin for a home-born slave: in short, someone who did not necessarily speak Latin, but who spoke a "home" language.

254. VICAR c. The vicar is a substitute, not in the sense of someone less worthy, but in the sense of someone who represents a higher authority.

255. VOLT c. This one is here for the nonscience majors. Along with many others, Volta had the distinction of having his discovery named for him, thus passing into the language.

256. WASSAIL c. This is the cognate, or the equivalent, of numerous toasts around the world: to life; good health; long life; and so on.

257. WISTARIA c. This word was inadvertently spelled wrong by Thomas Nuttall, the English gardener who named it after Wistar. Nuttall spelled it "wisteria," but the name of the eponymous doctor was Wistar, so "wistaria" is the correct spelling.

258. WORRY a. From the Old German for strangling: the immediacy of this derivation will be apparent to anyone who has had a major worry.

259. WRENCH a. It comes from the old word meaning "to de-

ceive," apparently from the context in which wrench is used to mean "twist" and, by implication, a twisty way of behaving.

260. XYLOPHONE   b.   It is from the Greek. This instrument seems to have existed, in one form or another, since people first made recognizable music.

261. YACHT   c.   The source is the original word "to hunt." These sleek ships, which are now a symbol of luxury, were once the fastest boats around, so they were apparently used for hunting down prey.

262. YTTRIUM   c.   Ytterby, in Sweden, is indeed the quarry where this rare earth was first identified.

263. ZEAL   c.   It can be traced back to the Greek, meaning "to boil" (with fervor, obviously). The Zealots were not a Greek group at all, despite their name. So if you are zealous, you are burning with whatever cause you are espousing.

264. ZINNIA   a.   Zinn named the flower after himself, as was the custom with many biologists. Bougainville, while not a biologist, assured himself at least temporary fame and immortality the same way.

2

"THAT'S NOT ENGLISH!"

Stories abound of faux pas in restaurants. There was the would-be gourmet who, when dining with friends, pointed to the most elaborate item on the menu and said to the waiter, "I see that dish is new. Whatever it is, please, serve it to us." The waiter's retort was short and sweet. "Sorry sir, that's the maître d'hôtel." This chapter won't save you from that kind of mistake—your own common sense should tell you to ask if you are absolutely unsure about a dish. You really don't want three courses of soup.

There is one step, though, that helps. Many dishes have a principal ingredient that gives them their name. In the chapter that follows, we have collected over thirty of these well-known dishes, provided a brief derivation of the name, and provided a quiz about the contents. When you've finished, you will at least know if you are going to get steak or carrots, which is some help; and you will have picked up choice morsels, not of food, but of food information, with which to start the dinner-table conversation.

The second half of the chapter is equally cultural, but not gastronomic. That portion consists of the Latin or French, or possibly Greek or German, abbreviations and references that pepper manuscripts and some conversations. You shouldn't use a foreign phrase or expression when a perfectly good English one exists (all too often it just sounds affected). But there are many, besides e.g. and i.e., that you run into all the time, such as op. cit., enfant terrible, and Zeitgeist. There are also some non-English words that have absolutely no English equivalent, or for which the English equivalent would take up a page, while the other language takes one word. A good example is *Schaudenfreud,* which is a malicious pleasure in someone else's misfortune or discomfiture. A direct example might be a practical joke a disliked coworker tried to play on you, but which misfired and actually happened to the boss, who has no sense of humor. You would be feeling *Schauden-freud* as your much-disliked colleague was called into the boss's office. Try to say that in one word in English. (This process works both ways, of course. The poor Frenchman has no way of saying one of the loveliest of English words, "home." It simply does not exist. There can be no songs in French about "Home, Sweet Home"; *domicile,* yes; *maison,* yes; at home where I live, yes; but nothing with the emotional connotations of home as we know it.)

So, as you take off on this culinary and linguistic voyage, Bon Voyage and Bon Appetit.

WHO'S THAT ON MY PLATE?

1. **ARGENTEUIL** This is a town in which a particularly famous item is reputed to be the best in all of France. The French, in general, do not consider anything but French produce to come under the rubric "the best." You would find that any dish labeled "Argenteuil" would contain:
   a. Miniature artichokes
   b. Asparagus
   c. Peaches

2. **AURORE** This particular effect, or sauce, or dish is named after Aurora, the goddess of the dawn. It will normally contain:
   a. Eggs that were just laid that morning
   b. Fruit with the morning dew still on it
   c. Tomatoes

3. **BÉARNAISE** Something prepared in the style of Béarn, in France. Anything you get with this title will normally include:
   a. Shallots and tarragon (plus many other items, but always those two)
   b. Red wine from that region
   c. Rice, as Béarn is in the south of France, where rice is grown

4. **BÉCHAMEL** This famous sauce, named after Louis de Béchamel, has certain very special characteristics:
   a. Green peas and red wine
   b. Potatoes and cream
   c. A white sauce with milk, onions, and often a clove

5. **BERCY** Named after a town in France, but the connection isn't obvious. This is one of the more commonly used sauces, including:
   a. White wine and shallots
   b. Red wine and small white onions
   c. Cantal cheese, exclusively

6. **BILLI-BI** This is a soup named after William B. Leeds, an American tin executive and magnate, in whose honor the soup was made at Maxim's. Because in French *B* is written phonetically as "bi," the soup turned into Billi-bi. Mr. Leeds enjoyed his soup, made of:
   a. Truffles and asparagus

    b.   Oxtails

    c.   Mussels

7. **CESAR SALAD (or CAESAR)** Now international but, according to most authorities, developed by Cesar Cardini in his restaurant in Tijuana, Mexico (please, note it is *not* Tia Juana, and shouldn't have that extra *a*). It usually involves:

    a.   Chili peppers and avocados

    b.   Almost raw eggs, garlic, and anchovies

    c.   Corn and Mexican beans in a hot sauce

8. **CHANTILLY** Along with being the name of a lovely racetrack and an exquisite chateau, Chantilly is a particularly fancy dessert in and of itself, also an accompaniment to other desserts. It is:

    a.   Fresh raspberries strained and made into a sauce

    b.   Tangerine sections cooked in syrup and sometimes served over ice cream or ices, or plain cake

    c.   Sweetened whipped cream with vanilla flavoring

9. **CHATEAUBRIAND** Though known for his place in history, Chateaubriand lives on in the cookbooks for a particular way he developed of cooking the steak, which is no longer made that way but still bears his name. His method was:

    a.   The steak was cooked covered with salt, which formed a crust and was broken off before serving

    b.   The steak was cooked between two other steaks, which were charred and then thrown away, only the middle steak being eaten

    c.   The steak was baked in a pastry crust

10. **CLAMART** This little town in France is well known for one product, which usually appears in dishes of this name:

    a.   Specially smoked hams

    b.   Very young green peas

    c.   A particular kind of young chicken

11. **DEMI-DEUIL** This style of preparation means "in half-mourning." It is not common, but it does occur in restaurants where the specialty is chicken. The chicken will arrive:

    a.   With half of it cooked as brown as possible, and half of it white meat

    b.   With the white meat covered with a dark brown sauce

c.   With slices of black truffle stuffed under the skin so that the black shows through the white skin

12.   **D'UXELLES**   La Varenne, the famous French chef after whom a noted cooking school has been named, developed this dish for his employer, the marquis d'Uxelles. It always contains:

a.   Mushrooms and onions, cooked down

b.   Crayfish, pounded to a paste

c.   Tomato concasse (pureed, strained)

13.   **FLORENTINE**   There is one ingredient that will always be found in any dish with "Florentine" in its name. It is a constant:

a.   Always lobster

b.   Always veal

c.   Always spinach

14.   **MAIDS OF HONOR**   You are most apt to find this delicacy in England, on the dessert menu. If you order it you will get:

a.   Lemon pie

b.   Baked apples with honey

c.   Small tartlets, lemon, almond, and cheese

15.   **À LA MAISON**   This item is extremely common on the menus of most restaurants. When you order anything "à la maison," you have a right to expect:

a.   That the item will contain beef juice

b.   That the food will be enclosed in a pastry crust

c.   That you should have asked in advance, as the expression means "house style" and can be anything at all, from steak with a special butter sauce to something smothered in kiwi fruit, ginger, and vinegar sauce

16.   **MAYONNAISE**   This familiar and useful sauce was developed by the chef of marshal de Richelieu at the Battle of Mahon and named for the occasion. It must always contain:

a.   Vinegar and sugar

b.   Egg yolks and oil

c.   Cream and eggs

17.   **MARENGO**   This name is usually a description of chicken, as that is all that was left after the Battle of Marengo, when Napoleon's chef tried to prepare dinner for the emperor. It contains:

a.   Wood mushrooms and forest ferns

    b. Plain boiled chicken, because that is all there was

    c. Tomatoes and mushrooms (though later additions seem to have been incorporated)

18. **MARGUERY (filet of sole)**   The Café de Marguery made its reputation on this dish (see the complete story in the answer). It has some unusual ingredients. What are they?

    a. Whipped cream and squeezed onion juice

    b. Ground lobster in the sauce

    c. Fish stock, mussel stock, and three-quarters of a pound of butter for each portion

19. **À LA MEUNIÈRE**   This phrase means "in the style of the miller's wife," but what does it mean if a fish is prepared in this style?

    a. Cooked in pure water from the millstream

    b. Baked in a crust made from milled flour

    c. Covered with flour and sauteed

20. **MONT BLANC**   This delicious dessert has two major ingredients. They are:

    a. Chocolate ice cream and vanilla sauce

    b. Chocolate cake, with whipped cream atop

    c. Chestnut puree and whipped cream

21. **MIMOSA**   While this is a flower, the name is often applied to a garnish for food. (It's also an orange juice and champagne cocktail, reputed to be the favorite at Buckingham Palace, but that story is rumor.) The garnish consists of:

    a. Candied mimosa blossoms on dessert

    b. Chopped white of hardboiled eggs to simulate mimosa flowers

    c. Sweetened with orange juice

22. **NAPOLEON**   This dessert is called a Napoleon in this country for unknown reasons. If you ask for a Napoleon in France you will get a good hearty laugh and a stare of bewilderment. What is this pastry called in France?

    a. Impératrice

    b. Mille-feuille

    c. Bonaparte

23. **NEWBURG** This fancy chafing-dish preparation, though originally used for lobster, is now used for shrimp, mussels, and other crustaceans. What are its chief ingredients?

    a. Shallots, Madeira, cream, and sometimes a small amount of tomato paste

    b. Hollandaise sauce with whipped cream beaten in

    c. Heavy cream and lobster stock

24. **À LA NORMANDE** This means "in the style of Normandy." There are several garnishes that use this name, but in the United States, you can expect to find:

    a. Some sort of fish in the preparation

    b. Apples and/or applejack (Calvados), and cream

    c. Normandy cheeses, typically Camembert

25. **PARMENTIER** This is named after a famous Frenchman who had an enormous influence on one French food. What was it?

    a. Beefsteak, which he learned how to feed better in order to make juicier steaks

    b. Potatoes, which he introduced and popularized

    c. Frogs' legs, which he was the first to cook and eat

26. **PERIGOURDINE** This means "in the style of Périgord," a section of France. It specializes in:

    a. Cheeses, especially the odorous ones

    b. Rice, for all dishes called "Périgourdine" contain rice

    c. Truffles, which are a major export of the region

27. **PETIT FOURS** These are those tiny cakes, usually cut in diamonds or squares, from a larger sheet and iced in rather poisonous pastel shades. Why are they called petit fours?

    a. Because a normal sheet cake will make four of them

    b. Because they were baked in the small oven (*petit four*), while the big one was cooking other food

    c. Because *four* is the old word for "cake," and these were small ones

28. **ROCKEFELLER**   Usually used to mean oysters prepared in a certain way. The oysters were considered to be so rich that this name was equivalent to saying "millionaire oysters."
    a. Spinach and pernod, as far as can be determined by others, but it is a family secret at Antoine's restaurant in New Orleans
    b. Truffles and foie gras
    c. Champagne sauce

29. **ROSSINI**   This sauce is commonly met with as a garnish for filet mignon (*tournedos*—which are pronounced, by the way, with the accent on the first syllable, not like the hurricane). It was named after the composer, who was very fond of it, and contains:
    a. Foie gras and truffles
    b. Red wine and truffles
    c. Red wine and crepes

30. **ST. GERMAIN**   This soup (or garnish) was named after a French town famous for this produce. What is it?
    a. Peas
    b. A special type of seedless cherry that is very much in demand for fruit tarts
    c. The very long European cucumbers

31. **SOUBISE**   A sauce invented by Marin, maître d'hôtel, at that time the title of "master of the household," for the marshal of Soubise. What is its chief ingredient?
    a. The newly developed potato
    b. The newly introduced tomato, a great novelty
    c. Onions and sometimes rice

32. **SUZETTE (CREPE)**   This flaming dessert, it is claimed by Charpentier, the famous French chef, was invented by him for the prince of Wales. What flavor is it?
    a. Crème de cacao and chocolate flavoring
    b. Crème de menthe and mint-flavored sauce
    c. Orange shreds and an orange-flavored liqueur

33. **TARTARE**   This is usually on the menu as steak tartare, but the adjective "tartare" has also been seen recently applied to such things as tuna. What does it mean?

    a.   In the style of the Tartars, namely, with sour cream

    b.   Raw, with garnishes of raw egg, onions, and so on

    c.   Russian style, with a vodka sauce

34. **VICHYSSOISE**   This soup was invented by Chef Louis Diat, one of the all-time greats. He said he made it from the memories of his mother's kitchen in rural France. It can be served hot or cold but is more often cold. What are its two chief ingredients?

    a.   Onions and chicken

    b.   Pigs'-feet jelly and garlic

    c.   Leeks and potatoes

ANSWERS: WHO'S THAT ON MY PLATE?

1. **ARGENTEUIL** b. Asparagus: in Europe it is possible to buy several kinds and colors of asparagus, white, green, and purple. The first ones of the season are hailed in all the restaurants at prices that stagger the mind.

2. **AURORE** c. Tomatoes: with a touch of poetry, the tomatoes turn the sauce a rosy pink, thus suggesting to the original composer of this sauce (Monsieur Inconnu) the rosy fingers of the dawn, which the goddess Aurora represents.

3. **BÉARNAISE** a. Always shallots and tarragon: many things labeled Henry IV also include sauce béarnaise, as he was born in Béarn and was very proud of it. It was he, by the way, who promised his peasants a chicken in every pot; and he was known, into what was then considered old age (fifty-four), as the Green Gallant for his frequent romances.

4. **BÉCHAMEL** c. This is one of the basic white sauces. Other things can be added, but the distinguishing feature is the milk, not water or stock in the sauce.

5. **BERCY** a. Shallots, white wine, and, if properly made, marrow in dice. You won't often find the marrow except in the finest restaurants. There is usually some meat glaze, too, as this is a meat sauce.

6. **BILLI-BI** c. Mr. Leeds ate in Maxim's frequently (he was a very rich man, obviously), and he loved mussels. This dish was invented for him and became so popular that it received his name in a Frenchified form.

7. **CESAR SALAD** b. According to Julia Child, this salad was invented by Cesar Cardini in his hotel in Tijuana, Mexico, a sort of resort for (Los) Angelenos and the rest of southern California, and it spread from there. She stated in one of her books that she ate it there in the early 1920s. The secrets are garlic, a one-minute coddled egg, and anchovies, plus romaine lettuce.

8. **CHANTILLY** c. Anything labeled Chantilly should have dollops of whipped cream with a faint vanilla flavor, though the vanilla flavor often exists only in the imagination.

9. **CHATEAUBRIAND** b. This method is reputed to have been developed either by the statesman himself or by his chef—

probability says most likely the latter. Because it involves throwing away two steaks for every one used, this way of cooking steaks is rarely used; but the same cut of meat, grilled, is called a chateaubriand.

10. CLAMART   b.   This name refers to a particular kind of young pea. To the surprise of some, no doubt, there are dozens of varieties of peas (Thomas Jefferson grew almost thirty types), and Clamarts are so young they may be eaten raw or cooked, pod and all.

11. DEMI-DEUIL   c.   Obviously, you are not going to find this dish on many menus. With truffles costing what they do, this form of "half-mourning" has gone the way of widow's weeds.

12. D'UXELLES   a.   This is a very popular garnish. It is in almost all good cookbooks, and the mixture is used to stuff tomatoes, crepes, and anything else that can use a mushroom taste.

13. FLORENTINE   c.   Always spinach, never anything else: when a French king married one of the de Medicis from Florence, she brought spinach with her, and it was called the Florentine vegetable from then on.

14. MAIDS OF HONOR   c.   These tarts, slightly bitter cheesecakes with almonds, were immensely popular when they w ere developed in Richmond, Surrey. There are all sorts of speculations about the name, but we really don't know its source.

15. À LA MAISON   c.   All this phrase means is "house style." If there is a really good chef in the kitchen, you will get something fine, but you have no way of knowing what it is unless you ask.

16. MAYONNAISE   b.   The two constants are egg yolks and oil. The oil was a novelty at that time for haute cuisine.

17. MARENGO   c.   Tomatoes and mushrooms are given by two reputable cookbooks. Others leave out the tomatoes (including Mrs. Beeton, writing only a few decades after the battle; still others insist tomatoes were in the original. The addition of crayfish to the recipe is slightly dubious. In view of the location of Marengo and the conditions there, it is improbable that there were crayfish in the immediate vicinity ready to be cooked.

18. MARGUERY   c.   The Café de Marguery in Paris invented this sauce. Diamond Jim Brady ate it there and requested Rector's,

in New York, to duplicate it. Rector sent his son, already a chef, to Paris, where he worked as a busboy and junior waiter for months before being allowed to work in the kitchen at all. He observed, tasted, and tried, and sailed for home with the precious recipe. The gala dinner that followed produced the remark from Diamond Jim Brady, "I could eat this on a towel, it's so good." It is not a sauce much in use today. It does require three-quarters of a pound of butter for each portion, or perhaps each two portions, which is not in tune with our tastes today.

19. À LA MEUNIÈRE   c.   The fish is dusted heavily with flour, like anyone working in a flour mill, and sauteed well in butter.

20. MONT BLANC   c.   The chestnut puree, crowned by whipped cream, is believed to look like the mountain with snow on the top.

21. MIMOSA   b.   That chopped white of egg, and sometimes even chopped yolk, are supposed to give the effect of mimosa blossoms. In the United States, it is sometimes served on a spinach salad.

22. NAPOLEON   b.   Mille-feuille, or "thousand leaves," in reference to the flaky pastry. It is absolutely never called a Napoleon.

23. NEWBURG   a.   Captain Ben Wenberg desired culinary immortality. He taught the chef at Delmonico's, at that time one of the most famous restaurants in the United States, how to make this dish, and it was named Lobster Wenberg on the menu. But he had a fight with the owner, who tried to remove it from the menu entirely. He couldn't, because it was so popular, so he got his revenge by changing the letters around to Lobster Newburg. At least, that's the story in the reference books.

24. À LA NORMANDE   b.   In the United States, you can usually expect to find apples (and, it is hoped, cider or applejack), and always expect cream when you order anything à la Normande.

25. PARMENTIER   b.   Parmentier popularized the potato at court, but the common people wouldn't touch it as a food. So he set up a special plot of ground to grow potatoes "for the royal family only" and posted a guard to keep everyone else from stealing the seed potatoes. The guards had strict instructions to look the other way if anyone sneaked in. As everyone wanted

the food served at the royal table, within a short time potatoes had become one of the glories of French cuisine.

26. PÉRIGOURDINE   c.   Périgord is noted for its truffles.

27. PETIT FOURS   b.   *Four* means "oven" in French.

28. ROCKEFELLER   a.   Nobody at Antoine's will give the recipe, and they insist it is *not* spinach. (It tasted like spinach to me.)

29. ROSSINI   a.   This is one of the richest of all garnishes. Rossini is reputed to have had an insatiable appetite for this particular confection and to have eaten spaghetti Rossini, eggs Rossini, and so on.

30. ST. GERMAIN   a.   Peas: these are not the tiny, special variety mentioned earlier, just garden-type large ones.

31. SOUBISE   c.   Onions, usually, cooked down to a puree. There is another sauce with the same name that also includes rice.

32. SUZETTE (CREPES)   c.   This is basically an orange-flavored sauce, flamed at the table over folded sweet crepes. Henri Charpentier claimed that he invented it at the Café Royale in Monte Carlo when he accidentally burned the crepes while making dessert for the prince of Wales (Edward VII), and that he named it for the young lady he was with. According to the date Charpentier gives, he was fourteen years old, and the story says he was the only one in the private room where the prince was being served. This claim stretches credulity to the breaking point. If Rector's son, already a qualified chef, was made to serve a long apprenticeship before he could even touch the food at the Café de Marguery, what are the chances that the management of the Café Royale, an extremely famous and good restaurant, dealing with someone who was not only a noted gourmet but also the prince of Wales, would entrust the cooking of his dessert to a fourteen-year-old all by himself? The prince was also a very, very generous tipper. It is far more likely that there was a platoon of headwaiters, waiters, and captains waiting on such a distinguished guest. Nice try, but sorry, Henri.

33. TARTARE   b.   The story goes that the Tartars, to tenderize their meat, used to put it under their saddles and ride all day. The minced mess that came out was edible (or so they say). Just don't ask for your steak tartare well done.

34. VICHYSSOISE   c.   Louis Diat writes in one of his books that he
     remembered the leek-and-potato soup his mother had made in
     her farm kitchen and attempted to re-create it in a more refined
     way. At one time, he stated, he was thinking of adding a little
     tomato, but it was such a success that he left it in the form in
     which it is now served. (Incidentally, the last *s* is pronounced.
     It is not *vichySWA* but *vichySWAZ*.)

BORROWED FINERY

The following phrases, words, abbreviations, and expressions are often met with, one way or another. You will find them in books and manuscripts, and will occasionally hear them quoted. Do you know what they are? Try the following quiz and see.

35. **AMOR VINCIT OMNIA** This phrase was printed on matchbooks at a wedding the author recently attended. It means:
    a. Love conquers all
    b. Long live love
    c. Romance is more important than anything else

36. **AD ASTRA PER ASPERA** This is the motto of several colleges and other organizations. It means:
    a. Work and hope
    b. To the stars, through troubles
    c. To the stars, with vision

37. **AD HOC** A phrase used to designate, usually, a particular type of committee or action. An ad-hoc committee is set up for what purpose?
    a. To deal exclusively with "this case" or a very specific situation
    b. To make specific recommendations, as charged
    c. To function as an advisory board for a larger committee

38. **ALTER EGO** A phrase used in speaking of two people who are close. It literally means:
    a. A changed self
    b. Another self, a second self
    c. To strengthen the ego

39. **AMICUS CURIAE** This one is often seen in reports of court cases. It means that the person so named is (acting as):
    a. A friend of the court
    b. In defense of the law
    c. As a disinterested witness

40. **ANTEBELLUM**   This phrase is often used in describing events or dwellings in the American South. (It is often, and erroneously, spelled antibellum). It means:

 a.   Because of the war

 b.   Before the war—specifically, in the United States, before the War Between the States (Civil War)

 c.   Of great charm, like the prewar South

41. **BÊTE NOIRE**   If you hear someone or something referred to as a bête noire, the person speaking means it (or he, or she) is:

 a.   Greatly feared, an object of dread

 b.   A black sheep, the bad egg in the basket

 c.   A nightmare

42. **CARPE DIEM**   This is the motto of several colleges. The writer also has it written on her watch:

 a.   Beware of today (it may be bad)

 b.   Seize the day (take the opportunity offered)

 c.   Unto us is given a day

43. **CAVE CANEM**   A sign that says this is painted on a wall in ancient Pompeii. What does it say?

 a.   This is a cave (wine cellar) in which wine can be bought

 b.   This is the home of Mr. Canem

 c.   Beware of the dog

44. **CAVEAT EMPTOR**   Obviously another Latin phrase, meaning:

 a.   Dog for sale

 b.   Let the buyer beware

 c.   This article sold with no guarantees

45. **CORPUS DELICTI**   This is often referred to in accounts of criminal trials. It means:

 a.   The corpse of the murdered person

 b.   The body of the crime, the major facts of the crime

 c.   Anyone who is involved in the crime

46. **DEUS EX MACHINA**   This tradition started in the Greek theater, but it means:

 a.   Only the gods can make things operate

 b.   The machinations of the gods are more powerful than humans

    c. The god from the machine—a reference to the fact that a god figure would be brought in (possibly by a machine) to solve problems humans got themselves into

47. **EAU DE VIE** In one form or another, this term exists in every language. It means:

    a. Perfume

    b. Spirit of life

    c. Water of life (brandy or spirits)

48. **e.g.** exempli gratia—another term found in manuscripts, where it is almost always just e.g.

    a. Thanking you for the example . . .

    b. By way of example, for instance

    c. Thanks to the particular circumstance . . .

49. **FAIT ACCOMPLI** This expression is ordinarily used when someone is justifying an action he or she has taken, in order to prevent anything being done to reverse the action.

    a. The action was justified

    b. It's all finished

    c. I've accomplished what I set out to do

50. **FLAGRANTE DELICTO** This phrase is often used of a criminal caught before he has completed his crime. What does it mean?

    a. While the crime is blazing, in other words, "caught in the act"

    b. Open delinquency

    c. In defiance of the law as written

51. **HONI SOIT QUI MAL Y PENSE** This is the motto of the Order of the Garter, a royal order that is bestowed in England. It means:

    a. Think ill of no one

    b. Evil has no place in this thought

    c. Evil to him who evil thinks

52. **HORS D'OEUVRE** Now on menus as an appetizer or canapé. What does it really mean?

    a. Away from, or out of the work

    b. Canapé or side dish

    c. Much work for little

53. **i.e.**   This abbreviation often appears to indicate a parenthetical explanation without the parentheses. What are the words, and what do they mean?
    a. *Id est:* "it is," meaning "in other words"
    b. Item established
    c. If explained

54. **INFRA DIG**   Short for *infra dignitatum*, which is translated:
    a. Standing on one's dignity
    b. Beneath one's dignity
    c. Worthy of dignity

55. **IN STATUS QUO**   When someone wishes to leave a matter as it is, this expression is often used, meaning:
    a. Leave it as it is
    b. In the state in which (it is or it was, understood)
    c. In a sad state

56. **IPSO FACTO**   This expression is often misunderstood and misused. It really means:
    a. By the fact itself (that is, something is demonstrated by the event that has occurred or the object that is present)
    b. It has been shown to be true
    c. As a result, therefore

57. **LA GIOCONDA**   The name attached to the *Mona Lisa* in Italian. It means:
    a. Mrs. Giaconda
    b. The Laughing One
    c. The Thoughtful Lady

58. **IBID.**   When used in a manuscript, it means:
    a. The same (as previously mentioned, in a footnote, for example), really "ibidem"
    b. Please check the source
    c. This is hearsay

59. **LOC. CIT.**   Again, a manuscript abbreviation, indicating:
    a. *Loco citato*, "in the place cited"
    b. Refer to another reference
    c. This is the original quotation

60. **LUSUS NATURAE**   This phrase is sometimes used both for praise and for condemnation:
    a.   A freak of nature—good or bad
    b.   In the natural course of events
    c.   Nature produces all things

61. **MEMENTO MORI**   This phrase was often engraved on mourning rings and brooches given to friends of someone who had died. Its sense is:
    a.   Remember that you (too) must die
    b.   Death leaves memories behind
    c.   In memory of the one who has died

62. **NOBLESSE OBLIGE**   A motto, at one time, of French nobility, meaning:
    a.   You are obliged to serve the nobility
    b.   Nobility imposes requirements—meaning that high rank involves certain responsibilities
    c.   Do not forget the respect owed nobility

63. **NOLENS VOLENS**   Sometimes used as an interjection to show haste:
    a.   Let's rush
    b.   Willing(ly) or unwilling(ly), it has to be done
    c.   I am not doing it of my own free will

64. **OBITER DICTUM**   This phrase often appears in reports of court decisions or judicial reports. It means:
    a.   It is as ordered by the court
    b.   A passing remark, normally one made by a judge, not part of a judicial opinion but more or less as an aside
    c.   This is said for the benefit of the person taking dictation

65. **ON DIT**   A conversational remark about something that has happened or is about to happen:
    a.   They say—in other words, rumor has it
    b.   The only thing that was said is . . .
    c.   There is a verified report that so-and-so said . . .

66. **O TEMPORA O MORES**   A famous quotation attributed to Cicero, meaning:
    a.   With regard to the times in which we now live . . .
    b.   Oh, what times, oh, what morals!

    c.   The times produce the morals of the times

67. **PONS ASINORUM** This one is said about a particular problem in mathematics. Literally, it means:

    a.   The asses' bridge—in other words, the dumb ones can't do it

    b.   The point of easiness—the simplest point

    c.   The pond where the donkeys gaze at themselves

68. **P.M.** The abbreviation for the time after midday (twelve noon). It is the abbreviation for:

    a.   Past midday

    b.   Post meridiem (meridian: the highest point of the sun in the sky for the day)

    c.   Past midnight, later misunderstood and the sense changed

69. **QUID PRO QUO** This expression exists in many languages and can be easily translated into English:

    a.   tit for tat—fair exchange—this for that, not usually pejorative

    b.   For money you get honey

    c.   Don't step on me; I bite

70. **QUIS CUSTODIET IPSOS CUSTODES** Every time there is a scandal in public office, somebody is bound to quote this one, which means (in the vernacular):

    a.   You have to watch the bosses

    b.   Who's in charge here, anyway?

    c.   Who's watching the watchers?

71. **Q.E.D.** As most argumentative people say. This abbreviation usually accompanies a demolishing statement and winds up the argument, or so the speaker thinks. It means:

    a.   *Quod erat demonstrandum,* "which was to be demonstrated" or, briefly, "I've just proved it"

    b.   *Quis erunt dogma,* "that's the rule"

    c.   *Quorum est demonstratus,* "a majority rules"

72. **SANS SOUCI** The name given to several palaces and country homes of famous people in France, seen also on British cottages. It means:

    a.   My lovely home

    b.   The charm of the country

    c.   Without care or, colloquially, the happy place

73. **SIC TRANSIT GLORIA MUNDI** This one is used to indicate the transitoriness of fame. Literally, it means:
    a. Thus passes the glory of the world
    b. All of the world's glory is vanity
    c. Passing fancies don't last

74. **SUAVITER IN MODO, FORTITER IN RE** One of our presidents knew this one, but translated it for the benefit of the great American public:
    a. Nobody ever got rich by overestimating the intelligence of the public
    b. Walk softly and carry a big stick
    c. What's good for General Motors is good for the country

75. **TABULA RASA** This particular phrase was once used by a school of psychology to explain learning by children. It means:
    a. Teach children to write early
    b. (The mind is) a blank tablet (and therefore you can make what you will of any child)
    c. Children have race memories, which tend to be erased as they grow out of infancy

76. **ULTIMA THULE** Used as a description in reports of early voyages. It means:
    a. The utmost limit (the end of the world)
    b. The ultimate strain
    c. The last word

77. **VERBUM SAT SAPIENTI** This one is often abbreviated to *verbum sap.* It means:
    a. Stupid people say stupid things
    b. A word to the wise is sufficient
    c. Wisdom feeds knowledge

78. **WELTSCHMERZ** This German word is a popular philosophical comment (among those for whom philosophy is popular, of course). It is:
    a. World study, in other words, comparative philosophy
    b. World literature, comparisons of countries
    c. World sadness, sentimental pessimism about the state of the world

79. **ZEITGEIST** Another German word frequently encountered in serious philosophical discussions, meaning:
    a. The spirit of the current time
    b. The decline in morals of the present
    c. An overall view of world customs

ANSWERS: BORROWED FINERY

35. AMOR VINCIT OMNIA   a.   The next time you see this phrase on a souvenir ashtray, you'll recognize it. Another souvenir ashtray slogan is "L'amour fait passer le temps; le temps fait passer l'amour," which means "Love makes the time pass, time makes love pass." Sounds better in French.

36. AD ASTRA PER ASPERA   b.   It is intended to be an inspirational phrase.

37. AD HOC   a.   An ad-hoc committee is a temporary committee, with a commission to deal with only the problem before it.

38. ALTER EGO   b.   It is often used of coauthors, or twins, or two very close friends.

39. AMICUS CURIAE   a.   He is someone who is disinterested, an adviser, and not a party to the case being considered.

40. ANTEBELLUM   b.   Although it *can* mean before any war, it is almost exclusively used in the United States for the years before 1861, in the South.

41. BÊTE NOIRE   a.   Despite the exact translation of "black beast," there is no implication of "black sheep."

42. CARPE DIEM   b.   It means "seize the day"—take advantage of opportunity.

43. CAVE CANEM   c.   "Beware of the dog" is the message.

44. CAVEAT EMPTOR   b.   This is the same word, "beware," but in the subjunctive, actual meaning. "Let the buyer beware."

45. CORPUS DELICTI   b.   The body of the crime, the major facts: it is also a misconception that there must be an actual body to prove a murder. A very recent case in California just convicted a man of murder even though the body of the victim was never found and the defense claimed he had disappeared voluntarily.

46. DEUS EX MACHINA   c.   The god from the machine: usually the term is used today to mean an artificial and contrived solution with little relation to reality.

47. EAU DE VIE   c.   Literally, it is "water of life." Visgbeatha, Scottish for whisky, also means "water of life."

48. e.g.   b.   It is commonly written and said only in initials.

49. FAIT ACCOMPLI   b.   It means that the act has been done.

50. FLAGRANTE DELICTO   a.   The criminal is caught in the act.

51. HONI SOIT QUI MAL Y PENSE   c.   The phrase is embroidered on the order ribbon.

52. HORS D'OEUVRE   a.   It means "outside the work"—in other words, aside from the main courses. Similarly, hors de combat means "disabled" or "out of action."

53. i.e.   a.   It can also be translated "that is" or "namely."

54. INFRA DIG   b.   This phrase is usually said or written only in the abbreviated form.

55. IN STATUS QUO   b.   Often it is said simply as "status quo" or as "the status quo."

56. IPSO FACTO   a.   By the thing or fact itself is the correct sense.

57. LA GIOCONDA   b.   The laughing one—in French, it is called the same thing.

58. IBID.   a.   The term is always used in the short form.

59. LOC. CIT.   a.   This one is also only used in abbreviated form.

60. LUSUS NATURAE   a.   The literal translation, "a freak of nature," should not be viewed as a value judgment.

61. MEMENTO MORI   a.   This custom was popular in Rome and also in late Victorian days.

62. NOBLESSE OBLIGE   b.   Noble rank is a duty as well as a privilege.

63. NOLENS VOLENS   b.   There is a story that this is the origin of the phrase "willy-nilly" as misunderstood by people who had no Latin knowledge.

64. OBITER DICTUM   b.   An obiter dictum is *not* an official opinion.

65. ON DIT   a.   It is sometimes used as a noun, "an on-dit" to mean "a rumor."

66. O TEMPORA O MORES   b.   It is found in his famous oration.

67. PONS ASINORUM   a.   Essentially, it is used to mean a difficult task.

68. P.M.   b.   The abbreviation stands for "post meridian" (and A.M. is "ante meridian")

69. QUID PRO QUO   a.   It is a fair exchange.

70. QUIS CUSTODIET IPSOS CUSTODES   c.   In short, the guardians aren't guarding.

71. Q.E.D.   a.   It is used to mark the ends of geometry proofs.

72. SANS SOUCI   c.   A fair number of British country homes are

called this—those that aren't Dunrovin, or Bide-a-wee, or something similar.

73. SIC TRANSIT GLORIA MUNDI   a.   When Gloria Vanderbilt married for the first time, one of the New York City papers, noted for its irreverent headlines, wrote: "SIC TRANSIT GLORIA SUNDAY." On another occasion, a subway strike, when the workers called in ill, the headline was: "SICK TRANSIT GLORIA MONDAY."

74. SUAVITER IN MODO, FORTITER IN RE   b.   Theodore Roosevelt knew the Latin phrase and put it into good, colloquial English. Literally it means "gently in manner, strongly in deed."

75. TABULA RASA   b.   This was one psychological concept that maintained environment was everything.

76. ULTIMA THULE   a.   Maps had this phrase on them. The American base in Greenland is called Thule. There is some indication that Greenland was the land meant on the original maps.

77. VERBUM SAT SAPIENTI   b.   It is generally, like many of the others, used in its abbreviated form, *verbum sap.*

78. WELTSCHMERZ   c.   "World sadness" is correct. The German word is untranslatable in English but indicates a generally pessimistic view of the world as expounded by some German philosophers.

79. ZEITGEIST   a.   This is another almost untranslatable word, so it is always used in German and not translated.

3

MISUNDERSTOOD, MISPRONOUNCED, AND MISUSED

There are many words that started off meaning one thing and have since acquired a totally different connotation and popular use: "alibi," for example. It has passed into common usage with a meaning quite different from its official, legal interpretation. What did it mean originally? What does it still mean, technically? Do you know? Read on and find out.

Pronunciation has suffered the same fate. There's a beautiful, romantic island off the coast of Italy that has undergone a linguistic change, at least partly because of its inclusion in the popular song, "Isle of Capri." Have you ever heard tourist stories about a sojourn in Rome that includes a description of sitting on the Via VenEEto, sipping a cup of coffee? Although it may not be wise to correct them, they were sipping their coffee on the Via VENeto. A certain movie star is probably responsible for the pronunciation of CopenHAHgen (as pronounced in one of his movies during the singing of a very popular song). There's a problem with that, however, as the Danes prefer CopenHAYgen. That's the way our language changes; and though purists have been struggling for years against such changes, generally they have been fighting a losing battle.

There is an entire body of science that covers the normal range of such changes over a long period of time. The brothers Grimm, of fairy tale fame, were actually philologists and published learned tomes on these changes. Did you know, for example, that in Italian, many of the Latin *l* sounds turned into *i*? Compare, for example, "flower" in English, *fleur* in French, and *fiore* in Italian. In French, the tendency is to put an *e* in front of words that once started with *s:* compare *estomac* and "stomach." These changes follow rules that seem to make some sense, and you can usually figure them out. But the rules do not tell us what to do with folk etymology, the process by which a word that sounds like another one is used for the correct first word: "sparrowgrass" for "asparagus," for example.

Verbs suffer both ways. Weak verbs, those which form their past tense by adding *ed,* are gradually forcing out "strong" verbs. Children are excellent at making this change: "I throwed" is sometimes more commonly heard among preschoolers than the strong form, "I threw." This disappearance of weak verbs has persisted through time. "Work" is a good example of a word changing before our ears. Do you know the past tense as it was not too long ago? (It was "wrought.") "Tread," which persists in stair tread, and some other forms, is dying. It should run, "tread, trod, treading, have trod," but this usage scarcely exists. One of the major New York City newspapers with a national reputation for accuracy in grammar recently printed a story that announced that an actor had "trodded the boards" for many years. This writer has heard several people say something like, "Oh, he's just trodding along," in the obvious—but mistaken—belief that the present tense is "trod."

So it has gone with English since the first Norman conquerors found that the raw meat in the kitchen had an English name, but what came to the table did not. What the servants worked with, they called by its Anglo-Saxon name, but what was served bore its Norman French term. Of course, the conquering Normans used a strong admixture of Viking terms, because they were only about a century removed from their Viking ancestors who had conquered Normandy (Viking from *vik*, "a fjord" of Norway, as in today's Narvik and Jarvik, not to mention many others). So it has gone with Old English, German, Greek, Latin, and French, plus other languages, including, surprisingly, Romany, the Gypsy tongue, which has supplied many of our more obscure words, such as *shiv*, for "knife." Of course, this particular source was more of a trickle than a major tributary to the English language, but it has added spice.

It is not surprising, then, that we have many words that are mispronounced and misunderstood. In many cases, they are words that bear a strong resemblance to something the speaker already knows or thinks he knows. (See "forte," for example.) In this chapter, you will find words that have altered noticeably, by assimilation, by the various laws of philology, by folk etymology, and by causes still unknown. Check the words carefully. You may find some that are new and interesting; you may find a word that you have unwittingly been using incorrectly; you may also find a word you have always wondered about; and you may find justification for your precision of speech. By the same token, you may find some correct pronunciations or usages that you cannot use, simply because nobody will believe you if you do! The author has been corrected, on at least one occasion, for a derivation that was correct by every dictionary, but which the listener had heard for many years derived differently in folk etymology: "cop," which does *not* mean "*C*onstable *o*n *P*atrol." Eight references fail to give that derivation, including the two most used dictionaries of American slang. (One popular reference attributes the name to the copper buttons used on policemen's uniforms.)

That doesn't stop millions of people from believing they know that that derivation is correct. Sometimes a little learning can lose friends and alienate others. Beware your erudition!

1. **AFFECT (compare "effect")** This word, starting with *a*, means "to influence" or "alter." It causes an *effect* (q.v.). Which of the following is correct?
    a. Her choice of one suitor over another effected her whole life
    b. The decisive battle at Tours affected the course of European history strongly
    c. He affected the transfer of funds from one bank to another very quickly and easily, with only one visit

2. **ALIBI** Colloquially, and in common usage, an excuse, usually in a court of law. It should be remembered, however, that its actual meaning is:
    a. I didn't do it—therefore it should be used only when pleading "Not Guilty" in court
    b. I can prove somebody else did it—used as a defense against wrongdoing
    c. The original Latin, and common legal meaning, is "I was elsewhere," meaning that the individual could not have committed the crime as he (she) was not present at the scene

3. **ALL RIGHT** Although the word "already" is correct, there is only one correct way to use the word or words meaning "satisfactory" or "acceptable." Pick the correct usage:
    a. It is alright to use alright when you mean "acceptable," but not when you mean "all correct"
    b. All right is the only correct usage and spelling for this set of words
    c. It is a matter of choice whether to use alright or all right

4. **AMATEUR** Usually used today to mean imperfect and defective, as the work of a beginner or nonprofessional. The actual definition is:
    a. Someone who engages in a sport or activity for pure love, as opposed to money or professional gain
    b. A tyro, a beginner

    c. Basically a dilettante who is unwilling to work at anything seriously because he or she is not really interested in it

5. **ANATHEMA** As generally understood, something that is abhorrent. Actually, the meaning is:
   a. A solemn ecclesiastical curse involving excommunication; someone or something generally accursed
   b. A person or thing who is strongly disliked
   c. Something almost like an allergy, that is, causing a strong negative reaction

6. **ANECDOTE** This word is often confused with the following one, "antidote." It actually means:
   a. A specific cure against a specific poison
   b. A long, rambling story with no point
   c. A short, personal narration of (usually) private life

7. **ANTIDOTE** As above, often confused with "anecdote." It actually means:
   a. A short story that exemplifies a point
   b. A specific against poison or against evil generally
   c. A humorous story about someone's private life

8. **ARCTIC** Pertaining to the area around the North Pole, and pronounced:
   a. ARtic
   b. Artic—both syllables equally emphasized
   c. ARCtic (with the *c* pronounced)

9. **ASPHALT** It is extremely common to mispronounce this very common substance. The correct pronunciation is:
   a. ASHfault
   b. ASfalt or ASfault
   c. ASHpalt

10. **CANARY ISLANDS** A group of islands off the coast of Africa, generally believed to be so named because of the small yellow birds found on them. Actually:
    a. The name was attached to the bird and the islands because of the yellow grapes that were canary-colored and that once grew there (wine industry wiped out some time ago by disease)

b. The early Arabs, who seem to have landed there, found the birds, which they called *al-khanar,* and the name became "Canaries"

c. There used to be a species of wild dog peculiar to those isolated islands, and the name is taken from the Latin for dog (*canis*), then later attached to the bird, the wine, and the dance that came from the islands

11. **CAPRI** A famous island off the coast of Italy, brought to the public's attention partly through a popular song. The name of the island is pronounced:

a. CapREE

b. CAPree

c. CAPEree

12. **CAREEN** This word is frequently confused with "career." We read of horses careening down the street, or a car careening. That word is "career" (look it up). What does "careen" mean?

a. To drive wildly and out of control

b. To turn a ship on its side for repairs

c. To race

13. **DAINTY** This particular word has changed its meaning sharply. It now means delicate, fastidious, extremely neat (sometimes connotations of petite, elegant). It started out meaning something rather different, namely:

a. Worthy and dignified, from the Latin *dignus*

b. Soiled, unclean

c. Large and imposing

14. **DECIMATE** Popularly used now to mean "cut down" or "slaughter indiscriminately." Originally, a specific meaning of:

a. To die from the plague

b. To punish by killing every tenth person

c. To count off by tens, for any purpose, but particularly for taxation

15. **DIMINUTION** A lessening, a making smaller. Often mispronounced. The correct pronunciation is:

a. DIMewnition

b. DiminYOUtion

c. DimINyoution

16. **EFFECT (compare "affect")** When used as a noun, "the result"; when used as a verb, "to accomplish, to carry out, to do": the noun is almost always "effect," not affect, except when speaking of an emotional tone. Which of the following is correct?

   a. The general affect of the war was a sudden inflation and devaluation of the currency

   b. The shortage of goods effected a marked change in the buying habits of the lower socioeconomic levels

   c. I cannot effect her behavior simply by words, so I will have to take action

17. **ETIQUETTE** Forms of ceremony; forms of prescribed behavior. This word has come a long way from its original meaning (in French, via the Old High German). In French it still means a ticket or a wine label. Why?

   a. It comes from the Latin for "label"

   b. It comes from Old High German *stekan,* "to stick," obviously to stick a label on something, but how it came to mean formal ceremonial is purely speculative

   c. From the French *etiquette* for "wine label," transferred from the serving of wine in the proper manner to all forms of correct service and then to correct behavior

18. **EXPATRIATE** As a verb, it means to banish from one's own country; as a noun, it generally means someone living out of his own country. Which of the following can be used as a synonym?

   a. ex-patriot

   b. ex-patriate

   c. expatrium

19. **FEBRUARY** Second month of our year, often mispronounced and rarely heard correctly. Are any of these correct?

   a. FebYEWary

   b. FebROOary

   c. FebYEWerry

20. **FORTE** That in which one excells, one's strongest point; also the stronger half of a foil or a sword blade. (*Not* the musical term.) It should be pronounced:

   a. FORtee

    b.   FORtay

    c.   FORT

21. **HEINOUS**   Often mispronounced, this word means an abominable action of great wickedness. The preferred pronunciation, according to four dictionaries and two etymological reference works, is:

    a.   HAYnus

    b.   HEEnius

    c.   HAYneeous

22. **HUSSY**   Today, this epithet has a most unpleasant pejorative connotation. One dictionary describes a hussy as a worthless wench. The word has changed greatly since its original development. It used to mean:

    a.   A playful young mare

    b.   A housewife, housekeeper

    c.   An apron worn by serving maids to keep their dresses clean, hence by association the maid herself

23. **IGNORAMUS**   Now, usually, a stupid person or one who knows nothing, from the Latin. Originally, however, it meant:

    a.   "We do not know" written on the back of a rejected indictment by a grand jury, meaning, we don't know if he (or she) did it

    b.   One who did not know Latin or Greek in medieval times

    c.   One who was ignorant of the law

24. **ILK**   Commonly used today to mean "of that kind." In everyday usage it would be said, "a ball player or someone of that ilk." That's incorrect. What does it really mean?

    a.   Similar but not identical to

    b.   Used correctly only for someone of a family bearing the same name, or for the estate of that family, as in "MacGregor of that ilk"

    c.   Can only be used for two objects of the same kind or species

25. **IMPLY (compare "infer")**   "Imply" now means "to express indirectly" or "to insinuate." It is used correctly in which of the following?

    a.   From the political column I read, I imply that the writer does not like the current government in his country

    b.   If I do not like what you do, I won't imply it, I'll say it to you directly

    c.   I imply from the circumstances that there has been some suspicion of this man

26.   **INCOGNITO**   This is another often mispronounced word. How should you say it?

    a.   inCOGnitoe

    b.   incogNEEtoe

    c.   inCOGneetoe

27.   **INFER (compare "imply")**   To draw logical conclusions from the actions, or words, or other activities of someone else. Someone else does the implying, you do the inferring when you think about what has been implied. For example, only one of the following is correct:

    a.   He inferred in his letter that he was looking for a loan

    b.   I inferred from his pleading tone that he was looking for a handout

    c.   The student inferred, from the totally irrelevant answer that he gave the professor, that he had not been paying attention

28.   **JEJUNE**   This word is often incorrectly used to mean "youthful." It really means:

    a.   Childlike in an uncomplimentary sense

    b.   Yellow-tinged

    c.   Dry, arid, spiritless

29.   **JIBE**   For some reason, this word is frequently heard as "jive." It has a specific meaning of its own. To begin with, it is usually given as "dial. U.S.," which means it is colloquial, and if you are going to use colloquialisms, use them correctly. This has nothing to do with jazz or lies, but usually means "in accord with."

    a.   His reports jibed with those I had heard

    b.   Don't give me that jie!

    c.   All of the correspondents submitted bills that jived to the penny, making the business manager very suspicious

30. **JODHPURS**   These riding trousers, named after their place of origin, Jodhpur in India, must rank high on the list of words normally mispronounced. If you want to fit in with the polo-playing set, you should call them:

a. JODfer

b. JODpurrz

c. JOferz

31. **KUDOS**   This is an odd word, directly from Homer's Greek. There is really only one correct way to utilize the word. Which of the following is correct?

a. A large kudo for Jennie Jones for her magnificent performance in *Salome*

b. Kudos are due Jennie Jones for her performance in *Salome*

c. Kudos is due Jennie Jones for her performance in *Salome*

32. **LIVID**   This means with white-hot anger, doesn't it? Or perhaps, red in the face with anger? Which of the following is correct?

a. Red-faced from anger

b. Black and blue, of a lead color, ashy

c. White-hot with anger

33. **MINUSCULE**   Everybody knows what this one means. Don't you? It means tiny, like mini, of course! Or does it? Pick the right derivation from these three:

a. Derived from "mini," meaning "small"

b. Derived from "minuscule" itself, which is a small, cursive script, as compared to *majuscule* (dating back to the seventh to ninth centuries and always spelled min*u*scule, not min*i*scule)

c. A corruption of "miniscule," meaning "small writing," now meaning anything small and insignificant

34. **MOOT**   This is another word that is almost always a source of problems. The original meaning seems to have been lost along the way and a false one substituted. Pick the correct usage from these choices:

a. The word "moot" derives from the old word for a debating meeting, and a moot point means a point that is debatable or arguable

    b. "Moot" is from the Old English for "a court decision," so that a moot point is one that has already been settled and is not suitable for argument

    c. Both of these senses are correct, and the word may be used in either context

35. **NICE** This word now means, in general usage, a degree of precision, refined, delicate. Its other meaning is:

    a. Finicky to a fault

    b. Foolishly simple, from the Latin *nescius*, "ignorant"

    c. Repulsive

36. **PANOPLY** This has rather suddenly turned into an "in" word, the way "charisma" was several years ago. It really means:

    a. The full range of skills or talent shown, as "the concert demonstrated the full panoply of her voice"

    b. The complete covering of shiny armor worn by a Greek soldier (hoplite), thus a complete covering of any kind

    c. A virtuoso demonstration

37. **PIQUE** This is a type of fabric when there is an accent on the last letter. It means "to anger" in one sense. It also:

    a. Means to excite the interest of

    b. Is used for "exciting interest" by confusion with "peak," as in, "that really piqued my interest"

    c. Means a state of irritation

38. **PREDOMINATE** To surpass in authority or in strength; to hold dominance over. The adverbial form of this word, often used to mean "the larger part of" or "the larger portion of" (with the implication of dominance over the rest), is correctly:

    a. Predominately

    b. Predominancely

    c. Predominantly

39. **PRISTINE** This word is so often used to mean "clean" that its original meaning has almost disappeared. Four dictionaries give the meaning as:

    a. Belonging to the earliest time; former or original state

    b. Sparkling white, white only

    c. A back-formation from "prissy," meaning that something is overly neat and orderly

40. **PRIX FIXE**   No question on this one—the only correct pro-nunciation for this phrase meaning "a fixed-price meal" (and American restaurants should say so) is PREE FEEX.

41. **SCHISM**   The preferred pronunciation of this word is as follows:
    a.   SIZm (with skism as a poor second choice)
    b.   Skism always
    c.   SIzm, with no exceptions

42. **SOPHISTICATED**   There is a difference of opinion on this one. Enough dictionaries give an unusual or uncommon usage for the allegedly sophisticated wordsmith or word user to need to know it (if only to demolish critics). The usage given in many dictionaries is:
    a.   Extremely polished to a false degree
    b.   Adulterated, deprived of naturalness
    c.   Complex and difficult

43. **TRIPTYCH**   Unless you are an art student or have attended art lectures, this may be a word you have wondered about. It follows the form of "diptych," a twofold panel or artwork, and means, of course, "a threefold panel." Some of the finest in the world exist in Belgium. The pronunciation is:
    a.   TRYptich
    b.   TRIPtik
    c.   TRIPEtik

44. **VALEDICTORIAN**   This is the individual who gives the vale-dictory address at a commencement. The individual selected is usually the one with the highest grades for the course com-pleted. But what does the word "valedictorian" actually mean?
    a.   The individual who has stood out from all of the rest by superiority
    b.   The individual selected to give the farewell address
    c.   The individual chosen to deliver the greetings of the faculty and students

45. **ZOOLOGY**   Not that you have to say this word very often, unless you are a zoologist, but if it should come up in the con-versation, it's nice to say it correctly. Is it:
    a.   ZOOologee

b.   zoOLogee

c.   ZOOlogee

There are a few others that it may be too late to save. When a president of the United States uses "enormity" as if it meant extremely large instead of a horrendous and evil crime, it probably means that enormity, meaning "wickedness," has passed from the language. Warren G. Harding single-handedly put "normalcy" into the American language. By comparison, Shakespeare is reputed to have coined more than three hundred words that did not exist before his time. The only pity is that when a word like "enormity" is destroyed, there is nothing to take its place except a rather clumsy phrase. A new word, which fills a need, is one thing. The *enormity* of destroying a perfectly good word that already fills a need is probably quite another.

ANSWERS: CHAPTER 3

1. **AFFECT b.** The battle *affected* the course of history. It influenced or altered, but didn't make the change of itself. The other two usages are incorrect. This is such a common error that it is worth learning the difference between the two words once and for all.

2. **ALIBI c.** The original Latin is the official meaning, "I was elsewhere." In popular usage, it now simply means an excuse and is often used in that sense in reports of trials by newspaper reporters who might choose to use a more accurate word. They might also, of course, refrain from reporting that an accused person pleaded innocent. You can plead "Guilty" or "Not Guilty," but not "Innocent." Pleading "Innocent" would mean you would have to prove you were innocent, and no one does. The burden is on the prosecution to prove you guilty, at least under the American legal system. Of course, a jury does not find a defendant innocent, it finds the defendant not guilty.

3. **ALL RIGHT a.** Although several dictionaries forbid the use of "alright," others list it as a variant. Time was when it was absolutely forbidden and listed as unacceptable, but lately, several dictionaries have given it as a possible alternative. Many books of style and usage prefer "all right," and some insist on it. In short, if you use "all right," under all circumstances, you will be all right; if you use "alright," you may have to justify yourself. Take the easy way out.

4. **AMATEUR a.** Someone who does something for the love of it, from the root word *amor*, "love," in Latin: it has come to be used in a derogatory sense, once in a while, for someone who is inept; and in a sports sense, for someone who plays without pay. But even the latter meaning obviously involves playing the sport for the love of it, not for the money.

5. **ANATHEMA a.** This is a much more serious word than commonly thought. It has been trivialized over the centuries and is now used, not incorrectly, to mean merely a strong dislike.

6. **ANECDOTE c.** This is the dictionary definition. In common usage it often means a short comparison based on an experience

similar to the one being described or a short, explanatory story involving a similar instance, told to prove a point.

7. **ANTIDOTE**   b.   This is the medical usage for an antipoison substance. When you need an antidote, you don't want an anecdote.

8. **ARCTIC**   c.   The omission of the *c* is almost universal, so much so that occasionally it is spelled that way in articles or on advertising signs. A few other dictionaries, notably *Webster's Third New International*, allow other pronunciations. Still, sound that *c*!

9. **ASPHALT**   b.   ASfault or ASfalt is correct. *Webster's Third* disagrees. No other pronunciation exists in any of the other four dictionaries I have checked.

10. **CANARY ISLANDS**   c.   In this instance, the birds, really finches, were named for the islands, not the other way around.

11. **CAPRI**   b.   Despite the popular song, which required incorrect pronunciation in order for the verses to scan, CAPree is what the locals call it.

12. **CAREEN**   b.   This does not mean run wildly out of control. It means to turn a ship on its side. The place where this is done is a careenage. How this word came to be confused with "career" is really not evident. No dictionary or reference book in the author's possession gives one for the other, and British writers are far less apt to use the wrong word. It is a mystery, but it is not a mystery that the only proper word for running out of control is "career."

13. **DAINTY**   a.   Worthy and dignified: we really don't know just when the change occurred, but obviously, the original meaning was still in use when the four-and-twenty blackbirds were baked in the pie. As you may recall, there is a line that runs, "Wasn't that a dainty dish to set before the king?" If you use the word "worthy" for dainty, it is obvious that the author of the lines was intending something quite different from what we mean today by "dainty."

14. **DECIMATE**   b., c.   Both are appropriate. It does have the sense of every tenth person, not of general slaughter.

15. **DIMINUTION**   b.   This is another instance, like February,

where the combination of letters seems to be particularly difficult to say. The pronunciation listed for (a) is heard far too often.

16. EFFECT   b.   This is one pair, "affect" and "effect," that is worth studying. They are quite different and have different meanings. Of course, to confuse the issue further, your "affect," in psychology, is your general emotional tone.

17. ETIQUETTE   a.   It's the Latin for "label," but in French it does mean "wine-bottle sticker," by an obvious derivation. It is not so obvious how it came to mean rules for correct behavior.

18. EXPATRIATE   None of them.   The first answer, as if the person were an American who was no longer a patriot, has appeared on book jackets and newspaper descriptions far too often. The real word refers merely to a person who has chosen or been forced to live outside his own country; it does not reflect upon his patriotism.

19. FEBRUARY   Dictionaries allow all three.   *Webster's Third* even offers (a) as the preferred pronunciation. Still, that shouldn't keep you from pronouncing it the best way, FebROOary.

20. FORTE   c.   If you are talking about the rapier blade or your specialty or expertise, ignore permissive dictionaries and eschew the final *ay* sound on the word. If you pronounce it correctly, however, you run the strong risk of being corrected, or misunderstood, or thought ignorant. The choice is yours—correct, or adjudged in error.

21. HEINOUS   a.   This pronunciation is preferred. Some newer and more tolerant dictionaries, which the writer does not like, permit HEEnous. The argument against HEEnous has been going on for more than one hundred fifty years.

22. HUSSY   b.   Originally this word merely meant "a housekeeper." It acquired its less savory meaning quite early, however: the *Oxford English Dictionary* goes all the way back to 1647 for the earliest rude use of the word.

23. IGNORAMUS   a.   This is still the first usage given in many dictionaries.

24. ILK   b.   Basically it means "of the same place or designation." To cite the *Oxford English Dictionary* again, in 1845 it was stated

that the word was erroneously used except for the identical place or family name, and so on. Later dictionaries are not as stringent. What most people mean when they say "of that ilk" is "of much the same sort."

25. IMPLY   b.   The basic rule of thumb is that you imply (in your speech or writing); and I infer, that is, I draw the conclusions.

26. INCOGNITO   a.   This is the preferred pronunciation in a majority of reputable dictionaries. Its pronunciation in this way matches other Latin words. Some more permissive dictionaries give (b) as a second choice.

27. INFER   b.   See "imply" for the explanation.

28. JEJUNE   c.   Probably by association with *jeune*, which is "young" in French, this has acquired the meaning of "childlike." The dictionary describes it in terms of (c).

29. JIBE   a.   It is colloquial, as indicated, but it is frequently heard.

30. JODHPURS   b.   We seem to have problems with words like this (compare "asphalt"). The *hp* or *ph* combination makes us expect the usual pronunciation, and we don't notice that it is really *hp* and not *ph*.

31. KUDOS   c.   Kudos, despite the *s* on the end, is only one thing and takes a singular verb. True, a few dictionaries allow that kudos may also be plural. But without the *s*, it is the sound of one hand clapping.

32. LIVID   b.   Again, contrary to popular usage, this means only black and blue, as in a bruise, or ashy gray, for a complexion.

33. MINUSCULE   b.   Basically, this adjective comes from medieval manuscript writing. The opposite is indeed majuscule, for "large letters."

34. MOOT   a.   This word must rank very high on the list of most misunderstood or misused words. It does not mean "settled," it means "debatable," and is rarely used correctly. Many books on usage and style have pointed out the error of using "moot" as if it meant "settled," but to little or no avail, so this may not do much good either. Still, now *you* know.

35. NICE   b.   This one is a bit of a surprise. General usage, in most dictionaries, gives the nod to the definition of precision, pleasantness, carefulness, and so on.

36. PANOPLY b. How this term got to mean a full range of skills, or talents, or demonstrations, is not indicated. It has turned into a common word meaning "extended range" or "full display of."

37. PIQUE a., b., c. The first two senses and possibly the third are correct, but not really all the time. If you are piqued, you can be angry or your curiosity can be piqued, so that you go to the dictionary to verify this entry; but you cannot spell either one of those meanings "peak" or "peek."

38. PREDOMINATE c. There is no word in any of five dictionaries I have checked that is spelled "predominately." All of them list "predominantly" as the only form known. This is another all-too-common error.

39. PRISTINE a. When snow falls, many writers give descriptions of the pristine countryside. They haven't checked the meaning of the word. More and more, however, it is coming to mean clean, new, and untouched.

40. PRIX FIXE As indicated, no question. When you see this phrase on the menu you can tell the waiter you want the PREE FEEX meal, and you will be charged a set price—a fixed price—for the total meal. This option has long been more common in Europe than here. In England, it is often called a "set meal."

41. SCHISM a. If you want to be correct under all circumstances, say SIZm. You may have to justify putting the *k* sound in.

42. SOPHISTICATED b. This definition certainly isn't what most of us mean when we say "sophisticated," and the common usage is coming into more and more dictionaries. The original usage, however, indeed meant false and adulterated!

43. TRIPTYCH b. It is one of those words that one reads in books but rarely has occasion to say, unless you are involved in the art world. It is pronounced exactly like the travel notes given by a major motorists' association, TRIPtick.

44. VALEDICTORIAN b. This word shows what happens when Latin roots are grafted to English meanings. We have a com-

mencement, which may be the commencement of adult life but is really the conclusion of that portion of academic life; and we have a valedictory speech that serves as a greeting, but is actually a farewell.

45.   ZOOLOGY   b.   Many dictionaries do allow zooOLogee.

PUZZLES AND GAMES

Now that you've learned all about Mr. Akademos and why a particular color is called magenta, not to mention the important background of such valuable words as cobalt and poinsettia, why not have a little fun with your word skills? A little word-puzzle fun.

Word puzzles are as old as words themselves. (One of the earliest known of such puzzles—a riddle actually—is the Riddle of the Sphinx: What walks on four legs in the morning, on two legs at midday, and on three legs in the evening?) The puzzles require little more than some word sense, some common sense, and a wish to solve them. And since you wouldn't have gotten this far if you didn't like words, the chances are that you will enjoy word puzzles.

In the puzzles that follow, you may find that you have worked out a more elegant solution than the one given. It is entirely possible. Solutions to word problems are limited only by the particular dictionary you use. If your dictionary includes many obscure or uncommon words, you may well find a slightly different answer. But that's the fun of puzzles like these. Not only can you use your wits, but you may also improve your vocabulary at the same time. If this is your first try at puzzles of this sort, just follow the instructions and use your brains and your reading skills.

As far as our friend the Sphinx is concerned, the answer is

"man"—who crawls as a baby, walks upright as an adult, and uses a cane at the end of his life. Now, on to the puzzles that follow!

The following three verse riddles are typical of the nineteenth century. (You can find examples of them in several works by Jane Austen and her contemporaries.) We've added an extra dimension: each word is also listed in chapter 1, so the clue preceding it may help.

Here's a sample to help you get started.

> My first is in blue, but not in glue;
> My second in old but not in new;
> My third in look but not in see
> My last in ask but not in plea
> My whole has leaves but not a flower
> 'Twill help you pass an idle hour.

The answer is "books." Read each line and the clue, and you will see how to solve these rhymes.

1. The first of this kind has somehow become a movie theater.

> My first is in read, but not in scan
> My second in pink, but not in tan
> My third in apple, also peach,
> My fourth in shingle, not in beach
> My fifth in two and also three
> My last in pour, but not in tea
> My whole a very famous view
> Shakespeare knew it, you should too.

2. The second has a Near Eastern origin, but it has come far from its source.

> My first is in dress, but not in robe
> My second in map, but not in globe;
> My third in mirth, but not in glee
> My fourth in plant, but not in tree,

My fifth in smart, but not in brain
My last in mask, but not in feign
The whole of me sometimes you'll find
On tables that are most refined.

3. The third puzzle of this kind may someday keep you in
at night.

My first is in chicken, but not in hen
My second in plume but not in pen;
My third in rose and role you'll find,
My fourth in fair, but not in kind,
My fifth in ten and also dime;
My last in wink and also wine.
My whole of French descent, it's true,
But now in English, Olde and new.

4. The last of this sort started out as a geographical term
and still is, though we often do not think of it in that way.
Clues are included in the poem.

My first in rose, but not in sun
My second in rise, and also run
My third in Indies, not in Hong Kong,
My fourth in East, but not in long,
My fifth in nabob, not in czar,
My last in tent, but not in jar.
My whole applies to those who are
Somewhat distant or afar.

Word squares have probably been with us a long time. It
seems to be impossible to find the earliest examples. In my
collection of puzzle books, dating back nearly two hundred
years, there are word squares in some of the earliest. They
are fun, but get extremely complicated when you try to work
out more than five letters. One man did a computer search
and came up with word squares of more than seven letters,
but using a computer is not as much fun as searching your
memory for words and achieving the satisfaction of a perfect
word square. For those who have not run into word squares—

a square in which all the words can be read down and across—here is a very simple example:

R A N
A L A
N A P

Once you really get into the business, you can spend hours working out five- and six-letter squares, a frustrating but enjoyable pastime, in the true sense of the word.

These word squares give you a hint, but you must fill them in along the lines given, which makes the solution both more difficult and easier.

5. Find a word square in which only the letters listed are used to fill in the rest of the square. Start with the word given and fill in the square, adding only the letters indicated: one V; two each of S and R; three Es, and one T.

C O N E
O
N
E

6. This time, starting with "mind," fill in a word square that adds one S, one D, two each of A and T, and three Es.

M I N D
I
N
D

7. For your third word square, only the letters are given, no words. Make up a word square using these letters. This will test your command of English—and your ingenuity. Of course, your answers on all of these may well be different—

there are probably several different arrangements of letters that will work.

Make a four-letter word square, like the others, using six Es, two each of A, D, and R, and one each of T, O, S, and N.

For a long time, a feature ran in a literary magazine that included verses with anagrams. They have been revived, and several of them are presented as puzzles here. You can rearrange the same letters to form words that will fit the blanks in each verse. A sample might be:

Jack climbed up and vanished from view,
His mother was sad, worried too,
"That __ __ __ __ was the cause of this strife
It is really the __ __ __ __ of my life."

The missing words, of course, are bean and bane.

8. Here are some harder ones to complete. The number of dashes tells you the number of letters to fill in for each word:

A visitor from far away
Gazed long upon the Scots __ __ __ __
When a __ __ __ __ ambled out of the wood
To the __ __ __ __ spot whereon he stood
Causing him shock and dismay.

9. Another one, this time with slightly more letters:

The chef said, "No __ __ __ __ __ of my __ __ __ __ __
I can't __ __ __ __ __ that dinner at eight
That mover I'd boil
In a pot full of oil
I'd __ __ __ __ __ in a way full of hate."

10. And still another one to fill in:

An actor who strayed far __ __ __ __ __ __
Found that his roles did not yield
Either money or fame
No one knew his name
"I have __ __ __ __ __ __ in my chosen field."

When you get up into the ten- and eleven-letter range, and even into nine letters, it becomes almost impossible to rhyme. Nonetheless, you can fill in the blanks in these sentences to make a sensible result. The same letters can be used to make as many words as there are blanks.

11. Many practices that should not occur have __ __ __-__ __ __ __ __ __ long past the point where usefulness ended because the errors were __ __ __ __ __ __ __-__ __ or ignored.

12. As the queen walked __ __ __ __ __ __ __ down the beautiful __ __ __ __ __ __ __ __ she noticed that the florists had supplied roses in error. They obviously had not known of her __ __ __ __ __ __ __ __ .

13. The commander in chief was reviewing his honor guard. "All of the __ __ __ __ __ __ __ may go," he said. "That means that one __ __ __ __ __ __ __ will __ __ __ __ __ __ __ ."

14. "Aha," said the sorcerer. "I have quite __ __ __ __-__ __ __ __ with my charms and spells. My __ __ __ __-__ __ __ __ skills are being put to full use."

15. "I was talked into __ __ __ __ __ __ __ __ __ __ __ ," said the young fellow. "I'd been with some of my high school friends who had already done it. That's what comes of __ __ __ __ __ __ __ __ __ __ and believing, instead of thinking."

Still another variant of this type of game is to see how many words you can make from a given group of letters. From *A, P, T,* for example, you can make pat and tap, not to mention apt.

16. How many common (or fairly common) English words can you make from the letters A C D E G I M R?

17. How many common English words can you make from the letters A E E L M N S S?

18. How many from the letters C E I K O R S T?

The idea of coiled sentences is not new. There aren't any new puzzles, just variations on old ones. The word squares that follow have one characteristic in common, however. They are all word squares made from multisyllable words. When you work out the squares, you will have an extremely complicated sentence that can then be translated into a popular proverb. Your puzzle is to work out the word square and then translate the puzzle into common, everyday English usage.

19. A sample is given below: start at the correct letter and move in any direction—up, down, right, left, or diagonally—using every letter once—to find the sentence.

S	U	A	I	R
R	O	L	E	T
E	F	I	A	M
R	I	S	T	N
U	O	N	G	E
A	T	L	U	F
O	T	A	E	R
T	H	L	Y	F
T	E	I	T	O

20. Another word square, but this time there is a twist to it that you may find a little unusual. Start at any letter and

move in any direction to unscramble the message. There is one null letter.

S	S	S	A	T	E
M	A	U	A	T	S
U	R	T	M	O	N
S	E	O	E	S	E
W	N	T	S	R	A

The following puzzles require both word knowledge and logic. They consist of lists of words. You must pick out the word that does not belong. The difference is not in the number of letters, the number of vowels, the number of syllables, word structure, or anything as obvious as that; but there is a significant difference between one word and the rest in the list. Can you find that difference?

21. cigar; calmer; sorbet; wined; beeches
22. octave; greet; patron; doorway
23. tangerine; regalia; analog; picnic

Puzzle these out! There are some puzzles that simply require you either to know or to puzzle out a word. Here are a few of them.

24. What is the tree that has all of the vowels in it?

25. What five-letter word can have the last four letters removed and still sound the same?

26. Find the words with the following letter sequences in them:

acca; wkw; nkn; hyx

27. The following words make up a calendar of the year. Each month is represented in one word—the definition is given. Fill in the missing letters.

J __ __ __ A __ N = This could be a description of a type of puzzle

F __ __ EB __ __ __ __ = Literally *or* figuratively, this one is hot

M __ __ __ A __ __ R __ = Now means anything small, but not originally

__ APR __ __ __ __ = Originally meant "with horns" but is now a sign

MAY __ __ __ __ __ __ __ = This food is named after someone moderately famous

JU __ __ __ N __ __ __ __ = A book division, a court distinction, or just plain childish

JU __ __ __ __ __ __ __ __ LY = Wisely, and usually well

__ AUG __ __ __ __ __ = Usually, it's something funny

SE __ P __ __ __ __ = Eve regrets this one

O __ __ __ __ __ __ CT __ __ __ = A six-car pileup on the expressway at rush hour, for example

__ __ __ __ __ NOV __ = Perhaps a special car, perhaps a super star

DEC __ __ __ __ __ = A garbage truck at six A.M.; a jet plane overhead; a traffic jam in Mexico City

28. Each of the following lines has three words interleaved. Each has to do with food. Unscramble the words.

```
C C A S M H E E M D B D W E A I R R T S S

T B A P N A G L E N R A I N N A E U M

B E G R S O G P P C L I C A O N L N I T A C H
```

The following three puzzles are a cross between crosswords, anagrams, and word squares. A quotation has been placed in the squares below. Spaces between the words have been indicated. You must unscramble the letters from below each line, decide where they fit (they are placed below their proper boxes), and reconstruct the quotation. Just to make it a little harder, the quotations are proverbs that have been put into extremely verbose language. Once you unscramble the puzzle, you have to decipher the sentence itself.

29.

E	A	B	A	A	A	E	A	A	L	O	F	A	C	A	E	I	I	I	E	D	A	T
H	D	E	C	B	I	T	E	F	N	O	M	O	C	L	L	T	O	L	G	E	L	R
I	E	F	I	I	L	I	N	R	S	M	W	F	O	N	R	T	N	I	O	P	S	
O	J	H	M	T	I	N	R	O	T	S			I	T	S	S	W	R	S		U	Y
R	N		R	T	N	T		S					T		V							

30.

A	B	J	E	A	A	L	I	F	E	R	O	F	S	R	E	E	C	E	G	E	A	R
I	L	T	O	C	T	R	I	I	S		O	O	T		N	F	U	L	S	S	N	T
O		Y		T	U	S		T	Y		N	U										

31.

A	E	K	C	A	M	E	F	B	E	C	A	E	A	E	I	T	O	U
B	S	S	T	F	O	I	G	H	L		G	H	S	T		Y	O	U
J	U				R	R		U	T		W	U	T			Y		

ANSWERS: PUZZLES AND GAMES

1. The answer to the first mystery poem is rialto.
2. The answer to the second is damask.
3. The answer to the third poem is curfew.
4. The answer to the last is Orient, and the poem itself contains hints that the word is geographical. Because the definition is valid only for Europeans and Americans, that hint is given too.
5. The first letter square is

$$
\begin{matrix}
C & O & N & E \\
O & V & E & R \\
N & E & T & S \\
E & R & S & E
\end{matrix}
$$

Of course, you may have come up with another solution. We'd like to see it, if you have a different square matching these specifications.

6. The second letter square is

$$
\begin{matrix}
M & I & N & D \\
I & D & E & A \\
N & E & S & T \\
D & A & T & E
\end{matrix}
$$

Again, there may well be other solutions to this problem. This is the one we found.

7. The third square was more difficult, as you had to make up your own words with no hints given. We came up with

$$
\begin{matrix}
T & R & E & E \\
R & O & A & D \\
E & A & S & E \\
E & D & E & N
\end{matrix}
$$

The anagram words are not as simple as they seem. There were rhymes to make the task a little easier, however.

8. Brae, bear, bare

9. Trace, crate, cater, react

10. Afield, failed

The anagrams in sentences are slightly harder, with only context clues. They are entirely reasonable, however, and can be solved.

11. Continued, unnoticed

12. Regally, gallery, allergy

13. Airmen, marine, remain

14. Finished, fiendish

15. Enlisting, listening

16. A C D E G I M R: decigram, grimaced. (If you can find any more, please write. This one did not seem to have any other anagrams.)

17. A E E L M N S S: nameless, maneless, salesmen, lameness, maleness

18. C E I K O R S T: corkiest, rockiest, stockier. (Again, if you find any more, please let us know.)

19. The first coiled sentence starts at the lower left-hand corner. It reads, "The totality of refulgent material is not auriferous"—or, in plain English, "All that glitters is not gold."

20. This word square was made from a palindrome, that is, a sentence that reads the same backward as forward. It is possible to start at either end—either with the S second from the left on the top line or the S up from the bottom left. There is one null. It reads, "Sums are not set as a test on Erasmus."

21. All but "beeches" can be anagrammed. The anagrams are Craig; Marcel; Osbert; Edwin, all boys' names. "Beeches" cannot be made into a boy's name.

22. All can be anagrammed into birds, fish, or other animals, except "doorway." They are avocet; egret; tarpon.

23. All can be anagrammed into countries but "picnic." The countries are Argentine; Algeria; Angola.

24. Sequoia
25. Queue
26. Staccato (also baccarat, baccalaurate, polacca, saccadic, and a few others); awkward; unknown (also blankness, pinkness, unknot, and several other words beginning with *unkn*); asphyxiate

27. Jigsawn, firebrand, miniature, Capricorn, mayonnaise, juvenile, judiciously, laughable, serpent, obstruction, supernova, decibels

28. Camembert, cheddar, swiss
    tangerine, banana, plum
    broccoli, eggplant, spinach

29. "Inhabitants of vitreous
    habitations will wisely
    refrain from casting pr-
    ojectiles of consolidat-
    ed mineral matter."

This sentence translates, of course, into "People who live in glass houses shouldn't throw stones."

30. "A totality of refulgent
    objects is not necessar-
    ily auriferous."

The translation is: "All that glitters is not gold."

31. "Be careful what you
    ask for because you
    just might get it."

HOW SMART ARE YOU?

The following twenty questions represent what you may encounter on an intelligence test, although we tried to make them a little more amusing than the average IQ-type question. Take the twenty questions and mark your answers carefully. Time yourself very carefully too, and work as quickly as you can.

TIME STARTED: _____

1. The day before two days after the day before tomorrow is SATURDAY. What day is it today?

2. What comes next, most logically, in the following sequence?

S A I B L C V D E E R F A G N H N I I J V K E L
R M S N A O R
a. P Y   b. B Q   c. R R   d. B R

3. What is one twentieth of one half of one tenth of 10,000?

4. What is the following scrambled word?

NNREAIVARYS

5. In the following examples, each set of symbols stands for a word. Study all three words given and the symbol equivalents and translate the fourth line into a word.

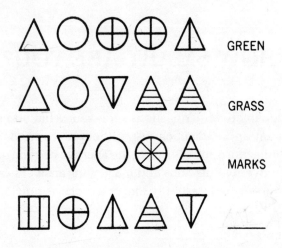

GREEN

GRASS

MARKS

_____

6. Which of the sentences given below means approximately the same as: "beauty is only skin deep"?
   a) Some actresses are so made up by the studios that you cannot tell what they really look like.
   b) Don't judge a book by its cover.
   c) Some people have prettier appearances than others.
   d) Good looks don't matter that much.

7. Which of the figures shown below the line of drawings best continues the sequence?

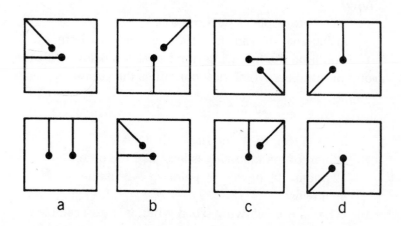

a   b   c   d

8. Canoe is to ocean liner as glider is to:
   a) kite b) airplane c) balloon d) car

9. Everyone at the Mensa party contest won prizes. Tom won more than Sally; Ann won less than Jane; Jane won less than Sally but more than Walter. Walter won fewer prizes than Ann. Who won the most prizes?

10. There is one five-letter word which can be inserted in each of the two blanks below. When you have put in the right word, you will have four new words, two on each line.

(Example: Place WORK on the line between HAND _____ PLACE, giving HANDWORK AND WORKPLACE.)

                    BOAT _____ WORK
                    DOG _____ HOLD

11. Tom, Jim, Peter, Susan, and Jane all took the Mensa test. Jane scored higher than Tom, Jim scored lower than Peter but higher than Susan, and Peter scored lower than Tom. All of them are eligible to join Mensa, but who had the highest score?

12. If it were two hours later, it would be half as long until midnight as it would be if it were an hour later. What time is it now?

13. Pear is to apple as potato is to:

a) banana   b) radish   c) strawberry   d) lettuce

14. Continue the following number series below with the group of numbers which best continues the series.

1 10 3 9 5 8 7 7 9 6 ? ?

a) 11 5   b) 10 5   c) 10 4   d) 11 6

15. Which of the following is least like the others?

a) poem   b) novel   c) painting   d) statue
e) flower

16. What is the following word when it is unscrambled?

H C P R A A T E U

17. What is the number that is one half of one quarter of one tenth of four hundred?

18. Which of the sentences given below means approximately the same as the proverb: "Don't count your chickens until they are hatched"?

a) Some eggs have double yolks so you can't really count eggs and chickens.

b) You can't walk around the henhouse to count the eggs because it will disturb the hens and they won't lay eggs.

c) It is not really sensible to rely on something that has not yet happened and may not ever happen.

d) Since eggs break so easily, you may not be accurate in your count of future chickens.

19. The *same* four-letter word can be placed on the blank lines below to make two new words from each of those shown. Put in the correct four-letter word to make four new words from those shown below.

(Example: HAND could be placed between BACK _____
WORK to make BACKHAND and HANDWORK.)

HEAD _____ MARK
DREAM _____ FALL

20. Which of the figures shown below the line of drawings
best completes the series?

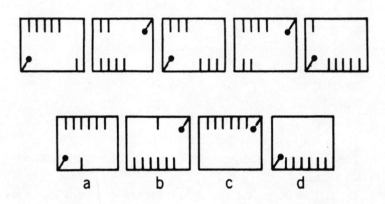

TIME FINISHED: _____

ANSWERS

1. Friday

2. a)   P Y The alternate letters starting with *S* spell "silver anniversar," and this sequence completes the phrase "silver anniversary."

3. 25

4. ANNIVERSARY

5. MENSA

6. b)

7. b)

8. b)

9. TOM

10. HOUSE

11. JANE

12. 9 P.M.

13. b) both grow in the ground

14. a) alternate numbers go up by 2 and down by 1, starting with 1, and 10.

15. e) The only one that is not an artistic work made by man

16. PARACHUTE

17. 5

18. c)

19. LAND

20. c). The number of lines goes down opposite the stick, up on the side with the stick, and the stick alternates from lower left to top right.

Now that you have finished, here is how to interpret the scores, based on a limited sample of Mensa members who took these tests. Score one point for each correct answer. Add 5 points if you finished in less than twenty minutes. Add 3 points if you finished in less than thirty minutes.

Total score 25: What are you waiting for? You're an excellent Mensa candidate.

Total score 20–24: You can almost surely pass the Mensa supervised test.

Total score 14–19: A very good candidate for Mensa.

Total score 10–13: A fair candidate.

Below 10: Everyone has an off day!

HOW TO JOIN MENSA

So now you've learned a great many new words, learned the origins of some old ones, and are anxious to put your new knowledge to good use. How about joining Mensa and meeting others who also like words? If you did well on the mini-quiz, try Mensa's test. Or, if you have prior scores from any standardized intelligence test, or equivalent, like the S.A.T., or the G.R.E., or the M.A.T., you may be eligible to join on the basis of such scores. Write to American Mensa Ltd., 1229 Corporate Drive West, Arlington, Texas 76006, for further information, or call 1-817-607-0060. Good luck!

In Canada, write to MENSA CANADA, Suite 232, 329 March Road, Kanata, Ontario K2K 2E1, Canada.